EXPLORING
embellishments

more artful quilts with fast-piece appliqué

Rose Hughes
author of *Dream Landscapes*

Martingale®
& COMPANY

Credits

President & CEO ● Tom Wierzbicki

Editor in Chief ● Mary V. Green

Managing Editor ● Tina Cook

Developmental Editor ● Karen Costello Soltys

Technical Editor ● Ellen Pahl

Copy Editor ● Marcy Heffernan

Design Director ● Stan Green

Production Manager ● Regina Girard

Illustrator ● Laurel Strand

Cover & Text Designer ● Shelly Garrison

Photographer ● Brent Kane

Mission Statement

Dedicated to providing quality products
and service to inspire creativity.

Exploring Embellishments:
More Artful Quilts with Fast-Piece Appliqué

© 2010 by Rose Hughes

Martingale®
& COMPANY

That Patchwork Place®

That Patchwork Place® is an imprint of
Martingale & Company®.

Martingale & Company
20205 144th Ave. NE
Woodinville, WA 98072-8478 USA
www.martingale-pub.com

Printed in China
15 14 13 12 11 10   8 7 6 5 4 3 2 1

**Library of Congress Cataloging-in-Publication Data
is available upon request.**

ISBN: 978-1-56477-989-2

ACKNOWLEDGMENTS

Creating is a very personal endeavor, but it does take a village. In other words, there are many people who help along the way, and I want to give really big thanks to everyone who has made the experience of writing a book fun. While I was the one working in the studio, or sitting at the computer, typing away at the words, there was a community of folks making this book happen.

A huge thank you goes to my family, who are always supportive, and all the people at Martingale & Company, who are amazingly wonderful to work with.

It would be impossible to single anyone out, but I would like to say thank you to my close friends who are available to chat and ready at almost any hour to kick around thoughts and ideas. Thank you to my friendship group, my design group—you know who you are—and also to the quilt artists in the groups that I belong to or have been a part of over the years. All of these relationships continue to bring light and joy to all that I am.

Additionally, there is the special group of artists that I call Fine-Feathered Friends. These three women have lent their art and their spirit to me in more ways than I can count. Each is an amazing artist and so much more. Susan Willen magically edits my words before they are ever sent out into the world. Cindy Rinne, with miles and miles of conversation, helps me pull everything together. Finally, Joanell Connolly is always there for me. It has been a joy to exhibit with these three women and to share my journey as a quilt artist with them. Thank you.

CONTENTS

FABRIC memories

For as long as I can remember I've always loved playing with fabric, and I have many, many bits and pieces of fabric memories.

One of the earliest things I can remember (maybe my first bit) was opening the big boxes of doll clothes that would arrive in the mail from my great-aunt Rae. Though I was never really one to sit and play with dolls, I loved opening that box. There were always treasures inside. She loved to collect used clothing and stitch it up into doll clothes. I found it intriguing that each little dress, skirt, or short set was perfectly constructed, and the fabrics were so like the ones of our daily lives. Everything was perfect, but on a smaller scale . . . much smaller. The fabric had been pulled from the ordinary and made into the extraordinary by her hand.

Another one of the bits and pieces of my fabric memories comes from one of my next-door neighbors, who was from England. She would invite me over during sleepy, warm summer afternoons, and we would sit on her front steps drinking tea while she shared with me the wonders of embroidery. There were incredible hanks of colored thread that were fun to just hold and admire, but with this thread, she would magically change simple white cloth into something wonderful with colorful, miraculous embroidery stitches. I learned to stitch beautiful (to my eight-year-old eyes) tea towels and earned my sewing badge for Girl Scouts. Memories from that time are filled with fabric, like the favorite dress . . . you know the one. Many of us seem to recall our lives and identify personal times through the clothes we wore and the fabrics of those special moments.

Looking back, I can see that the love and intrigue of fabric and stitching were always with me. During high school, when many of my classmates signed up for advanced drawing classes, I signed up for textile design. There Mr. Ramon introduced us to mountains of original Java batiks and taught us all the useful lesson of how to draw what we see, and to use nature as an unending source of design opportunities. Some of these designs made their way into batiks and stitchery projects that I created during those classes. They have formed a long-lasting fabric memory that stays with me more than 25 years later.

As I was growing up in the '60s, those lovely stitches and bits of fabric I created became a dominant feature on my jeans and other clothing. One memory that my mother and I still share is of the overall jean skirt that became the canvas for a large embroidered dragon. It was beautiful to my eyes. When the skirt had long outlived its normal usefulness, she begged me to throw it away, but I couldn't. It hung in the back of my closet for a long, long time. She couldn't throw it away either. I still wonder whatever became of that skirt!

Throughout these youthful fabric discoveries and the early experimentation with fabric, dyes, and thread, the love of fabric and the possibilities it holds was created. Though even I didn't realize it at the time, it would continue to play an important role in my life.

I've grown to realize that like the layers of fabrics I grew to admire and hold dear, life also is made up of a series of layers, many, many layers. Adding a layer may mean adding meaning and texture to our lives, and removing or peeling away layers can provide new revelations. Great metaphor, right? Well, I love using layers to transform my quilts, and my Fast-Piece Appliqué technique lends itself to the process of adding layers in many ways.

One way I've enjoyed using this idea of layers over the past several years is to start with just two fabrics. After some basic stitching, the top layer of fabric is cut away in places to expose the layer underneath. Revealing the underlying fabric in some areas allows it to speak out, and it also creates fun backgrounds for all kinds of embellishments. The backgrounds allow special treasures to be added that take "center stage." In this way, embellishments act as the key layer and help to move the quilt from what it is to what it might be.

Embellishments play a very important role in these finished pieces. I've played with or experimented with various design elements, innovative products, and techniques to come up with some of my favorite embellishments. But I must tell you, it's more important to simply let yourself play with the possibilities and have fun!

I've included six projects in this book that incorporate several embellishment techniques. The projects are all small quilt-art pieces, meant for wall hangings. However, all the fabric-embellishment methods you'll learn to play with along the way can be used to create any size piece your heart can imagine . . . and it will. Now, it's time to explore new possibilities!

ADORNING
ourselves and our quilts

Embellishments—colors, designs, and materials used for self and cultural expression—have a long, long history, spanning thousands of years.

Being a researcher by nature, I love the fact that the history of embellishments reaches back more than 30,000 years, showing how humans adorned themselves and their surroundings. For many years it was believed that we adorned ourselves in order to further deepen an attraction between men and women, but more recent discoveries show that people began to adorn themselves for other practical purposes.

Necklaces, armlets, bracelets, and belts made of metals, seeds, furs, woven fibers, beads, or feathers adorned clothing of all types, and they were worn not only to enhance one's appearance, but also for other deep symbolic meanings. These items were not only special and beautiful, but they also indicated one's religious, political, or social standing within the community, while other adornments were worn to protect the wearer from harm.

Embellishments Today

Embellishments, as we have come to know them, are generally accepted as unnecessary decorative objects embroidered, sewn, or similarly applied onto fabrics.

BEADS

Beads were among the first items known to be used for embellishing our selves and our lives, and most researchers agree that this is because of the holes. It may have started when our ancestors found shells, rocks, or pieces of wood with a natural hole; the hole provided a way to attach these pretty items to other things, or to string them together and make it easier to carry them along. It was only a small leap to figure out how to put a hole in various found materials.

Let your imagination roam over the possibilities of using shells, feathers, and beads on your quilt.

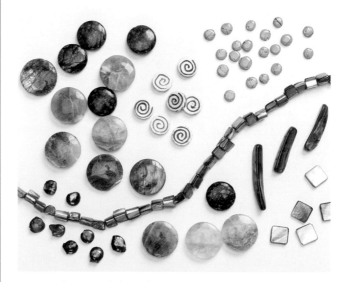

Natural materials have been used for thousands of years to create beads, and they're still being used today, as these samples of bone, shell, and stone show.

Seems rather simple, but the holes enabled those first embellishments to be easily attached. Even now, thousands of years later, we're forever trying to figure out just how to artfully attach that shiny new stone or some wonderful object we made out of wood, clay, or yarn to the fabric of the day.

BUTTONS

While beads probably were first in our embellishment history, buttons came in soon after, a very close second. Surprisingly, buttons were originally used for decoration only. They were not used as closures, as they are commonly used today, until a mere 5,000 years ago.

Small discs, typically round, buttons are usually attached to clothing in order to secure the clothing around our body, or for ornamentation. Functional buttons work by slipping the button through a fabric or thread loop, or by sliding the button through a reinforced slit called a buttonhole. (You may remember having to stitch one of these functional buttonholes back in junior-high home-economics class.)

Buttons are made from almost any material. Natural materials include antler, bone, horn, ivory, shell, stone, and wood. Some man-made materials are celluloid, glass, metal, Bakelite, and plastic.

Here are some marvelous buttons created from natural and man-made materials.

Every society has had the basic technology to make buttons and beads consisting of items from plant seeds to various stones, and many cultures are known for advancing the use of other various materials. India is known for the use of gemstones; the Egyptians, glazed quartz; China, stone; and here in North American, Native Americans were known for their use of turquoise.

Materials and processes to improve color, size, and even the weight of these original embellishments are continually being researched. A big leap occurred just a couple of years ago when the French found a new way to secure a coating of color to materials such as coconut and seashells. The coating gives these buttons the look and feel of glazed ceramic, and the color is permanent—unlike the dyes that had been used previously.

In spite of all this history and development, there are basically two types of commonly used buttons: flat, sew-through buttons and shank buttons. Even with just these two types, we have literally a world of buttons to choose from. As quilters, we can bring it all back full circle by using and thinking about attaching buttons not just as closures, but as embellishment.

Shank buttons have a small ring or a bar, with a hole, called the shank that protrudes from the back of the button. Thread is sewn through this shank to attach the button. There are also fabric-covered versions of the shank button; these have a separate back piece to secure the fabric over the button.

Some wonderful examples of shank buttons

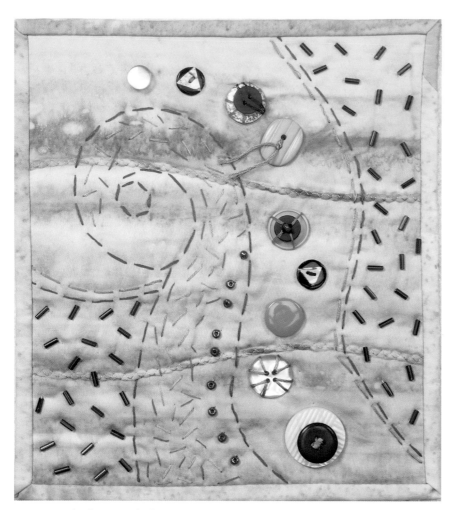

Flat buttons of all sizes, shapes, and colors have been stacked and stitched on this quilt for ornamentation, not function.

BEYOND BUTTONS AND BEADS

We've learned that to embellish something means to enhance its appearance by adding something decorative but unessential. Embellish is a synonym for adorn, but what I love best about these words is that they are verbs. Verbs express action, and there's nothing better than jumping in, taking action to make something beautiful, to decorate it, or garnish it. It's the added "extra" that makes it special, complete, extraordinary. Beads and buttons provide amazing embellishment opportunities, and we live in a wonderful time. We can easily go one step further in our quiltmaking by finding nontraditional materials that may already have holes for stitching them into place. Or we can add holes to countless materials, giving unlimited options for adding a special one-of-a-kind embellishment to our quilts.

At local stores, or on the Internet, we have almost immediate access to products and information that help us find new and exciting embellishments.

Flat, sew-through buttons have two or four holes punched through the button. Thread is sewn through the holes when attaching the button.

Examples of flat, sew-through buttons

A quick trip around your house is bound to turn up some fun objects that may be used to embellish a quilt. But, why stop there?!

FABRICATE YOUR OWN UNIQUE EMBELLISHMENTS

Fabricate means to construct or build from diverse but usually standardized parts.

My own journey into fabricating embellishments for my quilts began with my desire to find a way to make perfect ravens. I'm intrigued by ravens. They're very smart birds, and throughout history they have made an impression for good or bad on us humans. I love the various qualities that we've attributed to them. Ravens and the whole Corvid family (which includes crows, blackbirds, and blue jays) are known as collectors of shiny objects. There are many stories of missing keys or a favorite necklace showing up—in a tree. Ravens seem to be the perfect representative of me as an artist, and I continue to seek out new materials and methods to create the perfect raven embellishment (the shinier the better) for my quilts.

Seeking out and experimenting with new materials and methods are the best part of creating your own embellishments, and in the end you'll have something that is uniquely yours.

In this book I've included projects that provide opportunities for you to fabricate your own embellishments to adorn your quilts. Patterns and instructions are provided, and each project will teach you a new and exciting way to fabricate your own "embellishment stars." You'll learn along the way, adding information, techniques, and supplies to your own bag of tools.

Yarn, felt, and wool roving are just a few of the materials used to create fun and unique embellishments for our quilts!

BAG of tools

I've always looked upon my quilting life as an adventure, for it started as one thing and has taken many a meandering turn along the way. Each time I take a workshop, find a new technique, or see a new tool, I try to learn as much as possible. This way, whenever I'm creating, I can call upon this collection of information and tools and feel confident that I can combine them and use them for my needs. I've always called this collection of ideas, techniques, and tools my "bag of tools." R. Lee Sharpe summed up my feeling pretty well in his poem, "A Bag of Tools."

A Bag of Tools

Isn't it strange how princes and kings,
   and clowns that caper in sawdust rings,
and common people, like you and me,
are builders for eternity?

Each is given a list of rules;
a shapeless mass; a bag of tools.
And each must fashion, ere life is flown,
A stumbling block, or a Stepping-Stone.

Which will you fashion? I'm working on fashioning stepping stones, and the Fast-Piece Appliqué construction method I developed really steps in to help stitch creative quilt tops quickly and easily. (This technique was introduced in my book, *Dream Landscapes: Artful Quilts with Fast-Piece Appliqué*.) In this book we'll be using a simplified version of this method to create small quilts and use them as a canvas for diverse, fun embellishments that you make yourself.

This section is all about selecting the right tools and materials for your own bag of tools; having the right supplies helps you avoid stumbling blocks. I cover the basics here, and in each of the projects, you'll find a list of any special tools or additional supplies needed for that particular embellishment technique. Review the materials list found with each project before beginning, to ensure you have everything you need.

A dear friend of mine, Cynthia Catlin, created this special bag for me. While Cynthia is an amazing quilter, many of us love and know her as "the bag lady." The bag is shown here with many of my everyday tools. Other "virtual" tools have been tucked away in my head and are ready to pull out as I need them.

IMPORTANCE OF TOOLS

It seems to me that creativity lends itself to collecting, so as our love of quilting and creating grows, so do our collections. We collect important things like fabric of course, but we also begin other important collections that many of us don't really think about. This is our collection of tools. Many of us may learn the hard way just how important a tool is, and I have to admit that includes me. When first beginning my journey into quilting, I was guided in my adventures by a book that said I should have a rotary cutter, ruler, and cutting mat. Well, I really didn't think I needed the cutting mat. Needless to say, I did.

The tools and basic sewing supplies you'll need for the projects in this book are noted here. I have tried to keep the list down to essentials and offer you choices of things that you can use from stuff you may already have around the house.

By using the right tools and supplies for the job, your projects will flow together smoothly. The old adage about the right tool for the job applies to quilters as it does to all creative people.

FABRIC

The traditional cottons we use for our quilts are available in many colors, textures, and fun prints— deciding which to use is the hardest part. When you add in the possibility of silks and other nontraditional fabrics, the decision making gets even more complex. In the chapter called "The Perfect Background" (page 17), there's information on selecting colors and fabrics to create the right mood. If you choose fabrics other than cotton, make sure that they can be ironed without incident before using them in a project. Stabilize silks by applying a sheer to lightweight iron-on interfacing; iron it to the full length of fabric prior to cutting it to size. Silk-and-cotton blends do not need a stabilizer.

BEADS

Beads come in all shapes and sizes and are made from almost every material imaginable. I use them to add sparkle, color, and texture, and they also function as a part of my quilting. Just as I have a wide selection of fabrics to choose from, I also have a large collection of beads in a wide variety of types. I have always been fascinated with how glass and fabric work together. When combined, the textural contrast and visual impact create a magical quality that begs for attention.

Read on for a description of some basic bead types. As you're reading, remember that mixing sizes, colors, and even the types of beads throughout one area of your quilt can help to create desired effects.

Seed beads. Seed beads are round bits of various types of materials with holes in them, and because they come in so many sizes and colors, they make up a large portion of my stash. Glass seed beads are among my favorites, for they can be combined to create special effects and are easily sewn in place. They range in sizes 0–24, where the higher the number, the smaller the bead.

Seed beads come in a variety of colors, styles, and sizes.

Bugle beads. Another one of my favorite bead types is the bugle bead. These are tubular-shaped beads that, like seed beads, come in a huge variety of materials, colors, and sizes. The shape of the bugle bead lends itself to creating a linear quality. Bugle beads vary in length, starting at a mere 2 mm. The very long beads, those ¾" and longer, can easily break; use the long beads where they will not be disturbed or handled often.

Bugle beads come in a variety of colors and sizes and are useful for creating linear impressions.

Coin beads. I like to have a large stash of coin-shaped beads on hand. Besides the fact that they come in a variety of sizes and colors, they're round and flat. Because they're flat and occupy more visual space, they have more presence on a quilt, and because they're flat, they don't create a lump on a finished piece.

Coin-shaped beads are among my favorite styles.

Pressed glass or lampworked glass beads. These amazing glass beads have the most diversity of any beads I use, and there are more choices than can be imagined. Keep in mind how these beads will be used when selecting them for your projects.

Pressed glass or lampworked beads are very exciting and are the crown jewels of my collection.

Selecting Larger Beads

Large, bulky beads will create big lumps in your work and may keep it from lying or hanging flat. To avoid this, look for beads that will lie flat on your quilt. Generally, beads that are flat on one side are meant to be sewn on horizontally and will remain flat once they're sewn onto your quilt. You can find them by canvassing your local bead stores, checking out bead stores when traveling, or browsing the Internet.

DRAWING AND PATTERN-MAKING PAPER

Tracing paper is translucent and handy to use for creating patterns and in design work. Because it's easy to see through and allows you to trace images, it's an invaluable commodity in any studio. It comes in a variety of sizes—in pads and on rolls. A roll of 18" or wider tracing paper would cover all your needs, but as you begin to use it more often, you'll find that you'll want it in additional sizes for convenience.

SEWING TOOLS

Sewing machine. You should be familiar with your sewing machine, and it should have zigzag and machine-quilting capability. Be sure that it's in good working order and that you know how to change the stitch length and width.

Sewing machine feet. Besides a standard or ¼" foot for straight stitching, you will need a foot that accommodates zigzag stitching, a foot with an open area for the needle to move back and forth for the zigzag stitch. You may want to consider a specialty foot as well for couching over yarns. Most sewing-machine manufacturers market the foot as a braiding, cording, or couching foot. You may also want to have a darning or quilting foot available for free-motion machine quilting.

Sewing thread. Use a mid-weight cotton thread in a neutral color, such as gray or beige for sewing the quilt top. Note: The color should be visible from the top but not highly contrasting. You want to be able to see the stitching when you trim next to it. Use this thread for the top and in the bobbin.

Quilting and couching thread. Select metallic or other decorative threads that coordinate with yarns chosen for couching, quilting, and machine beading. When selecting bobbin thread for couching and quilting, select one that will work well with the backing fabric, as this thread will show on the back of the quilt. I personally like to use clear monofilament, but use this thread only in a metal bobbin filled no more than half full. This thread winds very tightly and may cause a plastic bobbin to break.

Beading thread. When beading by hand, use an exceptionally strong but pliable thread in colors that match the fabric colors where the beads will be sewn. My favorite beading thread is 60-weight lint-free polyester. This thread comes on prewound bobbins in a full range of colors.

This 60-weight polyester thread is perfect for beading. Keep assorted colors handy in a bobbin ring.

Embroidery thread. This decorative thread used for dimensional stitching is composed of six very loosely twisted threads. This makes the floss highly versatile; the six strands may be used together as they come off the skein, or they can be easily separated into any number of strands. Separated or joined with other colors, strands of floss help to create special effects. Embroidery floss is generally available by the skein, in cotton, silk, and rayon, and in a wide range of colors, including some variegated colors.

Pearl cotton. This is another type of decorative thread that may be used for dimensional stitching, but unlike embroidery thread it's tightly twisted and is not divisible. It's smooth with a low luster, highly praised for strength and durability, and is available in a huge variety of weights and colors. Pearl cotton is generally available for purchase in skeins or balls. The most common sizes are 12, which is very fine; 8, which is fine; 5, which is medium; and 3, which is heavy.

These are just a small sample of threads for embroidery-style dimensional stitching.

Basic Sewing Kit

Here's a complete list of everything needed to make wonderful background quilts, ready to show off the embellishment stars you'll be creating.

For Drawing and Marking

Soft-lead pencil

Pencil eraser

Fine-line (not ultra-fine) permanent black marker

Blunt-ended pencil-like tool, such as a wooden knitting needle

Wax-free transfer paper (such as Saral) in various colors

Chalk-powder or cartridge-type marker (optional)

Fabric markers (optional)

For Cutting

Paper scissors

Fabric scissors

Duckbill appliqué scissors

Rotary cutter and cutting mat

Long ruler

For Sewing and Couching

Size 80/12 or 90/14 sewing-machine needles

Size 80/12 or 90/14 topstitching or metallic sewing-machine needles

Couching or cording foot or open-toe foot

For Pressing

Iron

Ironing board

Pressing sheet (made of Teflon to protect iron and ironing surface when using fusible products)

For Layering and Basting

Lightweight cotton or cotton-blend batting

Masking tape

Safety pins

For Dimensional Stitching and Beading

Size 11 or 12 crewel hand-sewing needles (dimensional stitching)

Size 10 or 11 Sharp hand-sewing needles (hand beading)

Needle threader (optional)

Thimble (optional)

Small pincushion

Beading cup or tray

Be Prepared

I always keep a small hand-sewing kit with me. It contains needles for dimensional stitching and hand beading, a wool strawberry pincushion, a needle-threader, thimble, small scissors, and my handy chalk-liner tool.

the perfect BACKGROUND

With each project in this book, the focus is on making embellishments that are meant to be the special stars for each quilt.

In order to create the perfect stage for our embellishments, we'll use my Fast-Piece Appliqué technique in new ways. Using just two specially chosen fabrics, we'll create fun and easy backgrounds. This appliqué technique features easy machine stitching, which is then covered by yarns (known as couching).

As we create the background quilts to show off our embellishments, there are a couple of important items to keep in mind. The first, of course, is fabric selection, and the second is yarn selection. You'll want to choose fabrics and yarns while considering how the background or canvas will best show off the stars. No star ever wants to compete for attention or would tolerate fading into the background.

This doesn't mean that the fabrics need to be boring or not fun to work with. It just means you should consider the embellishment stars and pay special attention to the mood you're trying to create.

As part of the discussion in "Bag of Tools" on page 12, I talked about using cottons and other types of specialty fabrics, so make sure to consider all types when you're looking for fabric to create the projects in this book. Read on for additional information that will help you choose those fabrics.

GETTING MOODY

The fabric you select sets the mood for the whole piece. Have you ever seen a quilt that pulls at your heartstrings, or has created a place so wonderful and exciting, that it makes you want to jump in and be part of the scene? Any quilts that have affected you in this way have effectively created a mood.

Mood is another word for a state of mind or feeling, and artists use many things at their command to establish a mood in their work. As a first step, ask yourself just what mood you're trying to create. Subject matter and scenery make up a large portion

of the focus for setting the mood, but color can control it all. Because of this, knowing how to use color as a tool to create the mood is very important.

By combining colors in various ways, you'll be able to create different moods. Let's start by looking at the colors on the color wheel. Colors that are adjacent to each other interact with each other and create their own mood. For example, on the color wheel, the adjacent colors of yellow, yellow-orange, orange, red-orange, and red combine to create a warm, energetic mood. They also have a tendency to appear to move forward or toward the viewer. The colors green, green blue, blue, blue violet, and violet combine to create a cool, calm mood and have the appearance of moving back or receding.

Yellow, orange, and red create a warm mood.

There's a wealth of information about color theory, but we all bring our own interpretation and feeling to our color choices. Remember to please yourself first when choosing colors. Our interests, cultural backgrounds, and even where we live influence how we perceive and react to color. How color makes us feel is ultimately in the eye of the beholder. Color theory tells us that blues create a peaceful, serene feeling, but for some people, blue may bring up feelings of depression.

Does the combination of green, blue, and violet create a cool feeling for you? Remember that reactions to color are in the eye of the beholder.

Setting the Scene with Color

Here's an example of how color can control the mood of a scene. Think of a situation where the subject matter and scenery are the same, but where color changes, such as a walk on the beach at different times of the day.

At dawn, the sun barely makes its presence known. It's a calm, quiet time, and the colors around you may be mostly the blue of the sky and water. It's a lightened or grayed blue, and other colors affected by this light are also softer and grayed. All combine to create a feeling of calm and quiet.

At midday, it's entirely different. The sun is high in the sky, and all the colors around you are very true hues, making the feeling or mood very different. Pure colors feel awake, vibrant, and energetic.

As the sun sets, we again have a different scene due to the changing colors. At sunset, complementary colors come together in the sky and create a dramatic, climactic sky as the sun takes leave of the day. For me, the drama invokes a silent moment when I take a deep breath and gives thanks for the day.

With these descriptions I created small color studies for each of my beach walks. I used a collection of fabrics, yarns, and found objects to represent the colors I might find on my beach walk at dawn, midday, and at sunset. The environment and geography where I live definitely affects the colors that I see at each of these times of the day.

Dawn

Midday

Sunset

USING CONTRAST TO CREATE MOOD

Contrast of color and value can also help to create mood. Contrast, simply stated, is the perceived difference between two adjacent colors. Within each of the projects in this book, there's a dance that occurs between the background quilts and the fabricated embellishments that will be spotlighted, so contrast is a very important factor to consider when selecting fabric. The more contrast there is between the background quilts and the embellishments, the more the star embellishments will stand out and take center stage.

Color Contrast

When we first think of contrast, many of us immediately think of black and white. It's quite natural, for black and white adjacent to each other have a pronounced effect. When a detailed pattern is created using black and white, the effect can be very visually unsettling, because there is constant interaction occurring. This is commonly called vibration. Vibration also occurs when other contrasting colors are placed next to each other. For instance, complementary colors, those that sit opposite of each other on the color wheel, create high contrast when placed adjacent to each other. Examples of these include red and green, and yellow and violet. When the values of these complements are the same, they also will appear visually to vibrate. Vibrating colors can be difficult to view, so if you want a small exciting kick that is easy on the eyes, use small amounts of a color's complement. For instance, using the example of red and green, by using 90% green and 10% red you'll get a pleasing kick of excitement.

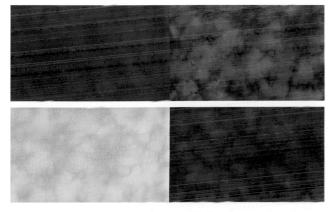

Here are two examples of contrasting color combinations: red and green, and yellow and violet.

Value Contrast

Black and white offer the greatest level of contrast, because they're not really colors. Hue is another word for color, and when it's pure (no white or black added), it can provide high levels of contrast. Saturation of a color describes how pure the color is. A color that's very pure is clear and bright. The purer the hue, the higher the contrast with other hues, but add black, and the color becomes muddied and dark. This is called a shade. Add white and the color lightens and is called a tint. By looking at "Setting the Scene with Color," on page 18, you'll see that the midday materials are closest to pure color and the contrast is more pronounced.

To further study contrast we look to value. Value is the degree of relative lightness or darkness of a color, and understanding value is a great tool to help set a mood. Usually value is described as light, medium, or dark, but this is only determined by having two colors adjacent to each other.

Do you want an eye-catching, vibrant quilt? Color is immediate, and it's what draws a person's attention toward your piece. The level of saturation and value in combination with hue will grab immediate attention. A low-contrast quilt may not jump out and attract immediate attention, but attention can be gained in subtler ways. Creating the desired mood is the ultimate goal, for it's the mood that will draw the viewer in.

I've created several versions of the same quilt background so that you can experience the differences that can be created by the use of color. A little bit of color knowledge can go a long way toward setting the mood for your quilt.

The first two examples represent high contrast and low contrast, while the second two are examples of how texture and pattern within the design of the fabrics work in tandem with color to further create the mood of the quilts. In each of these background quilts, I selected yarns that coincide with the mood created by the fabrics.

These dark fabrics contain black. Since the two fabrics are similar in value, the contrast is low, but the color and directional quality of the fabric patterns create quite the stormy atmosphere.

These fabrics contain highly saturated hues and offer a high level of contrast. One might imagine silhouetted birds flying home to roost at sunset.

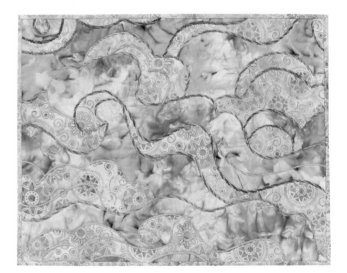

Although these fabric colors have been tinted, they create a high-contrast background due to high color saturation and the circular print in the blue fabric.

These fabric colors contain a good deal of white, creating tints. This combination of pale colors helps conjure images of early morning in the garden and creates a very soft, wonderfully low-contrast background.

DON'T FORGET THE YARN!

Yarn is a crucial item in the Fast-Piece Appliqué backgrounds; it's couched over the stitching that connects the layers of fabric to both conceal the stitching and add a wonderful design element. The best part is that there's an amazing array of incredible yarns for you to choose from. There are a few things to keep in mind while you search for great yarn, but first and foremost, everything you have learned about color in order to select fabrics also applies to choosing the perfect yarns.

One other thing I've learned about color and yarn pertains to variegated, multicolored yarns. These are some of my favorites. They help move the color throughout the piece, because they keep your eyes moving as well. As with the many types of fabric available, the many different types of variegated yarns today give different results. Variegated yarn is dyed in sections. Sometimes these colored sections may be random, and other times they're dyed in a set pattern. These variations will create very different effects on your quilt, so be sure to lay out the yarn on the quilt to help you choose.

In addition, consider the thickness and texture. Thin yarns are commonly used for needlework or crochet projects. When used on a quilt, a single strand of thin yarn may not cover the stitching lines adequately. The solution is to simply combine multiple strands. This will give you the coverage you need and open up the possibilities of combining different colors or textured yarns together for unique affect.

Combine different yarns to add color and texture while creating thickness for good coverage of stitching.

Thicker yarns may cover well, but extra-thick yarns may be difficult to stitch. They can create pulling or bunching as you sew, or your sewing machine may not provide a stitch wide enough to successfully couch down the really thick yarns.

When selecting yarn, consider thickness, color, and texture, but the most important thing is to have fun. Jump in and have a great time visiting local yarn stores, swapping bits of yarns with friends, and enjoying this new source of inspiration, for you *will* be inspired by all the lovely enticements out there.

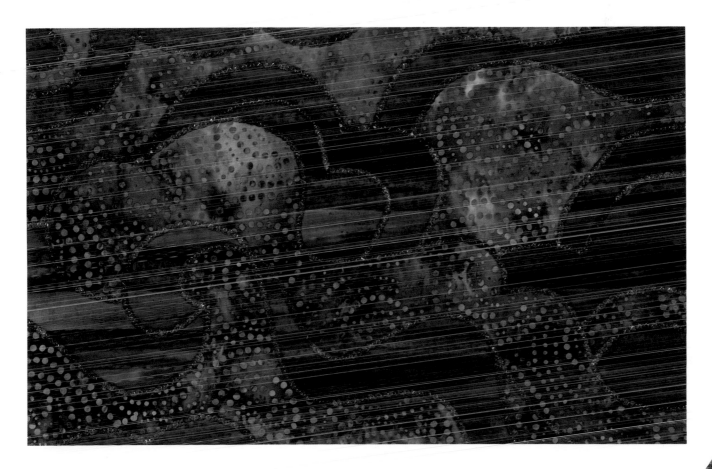

THE BASICS
of fast-piece appliqué backgrounds

Choosing color and texture should be fun, and it's best to let your design help set the mood you want to create and guide your selection choices. In the basic project that follows, I will show you how to quickly stitch up a two-fabric background using Fast-Piece Appliqué—all the while creating a wonderful stage for all the embellishment fun that's to come in the chapters that follow.

Using just straight stitch and zigzag stitch, you'll be pleased at how easily your quilted backdrop will come together. Zigzag stitching on your sewing machine is easy, and if it's a stitch that you haven't tried yet, you'll find it to be a welcome addition to your quilting skills.

CLOUD FLY-BY: A PROJECT FOR LEARNING

This small quilt will be used to show the step-by-step process for creating artful quilt backgrounds with the quick and fun Fast-Piece Appliqué method.

Finished size: 21½" x 17½"

Materials

⅝ yard of rainbow fabric for background

⅝ yard of batik for background

¼ yard of fabric for basic binding

⅝ yard of fabric for backing

24" x 22" piece of batting

Yarn for couching

Basic sewing supplies (page 16)

Tracing paper

Wax-free transfer paper

Blunt-ended tool, such as a wooden knitting needle

Duckbill appliqué scissors

Enlarging the Background Pattern

For this project and each of the quilts in this book, you'll first need to enlarge the pattern to the full, finished size. The pattern for the background quilt included with each project can be enlarged to any size, but the instructions are written for the specific size of the quilt shown. There are many ways to enlarge a pattern, including using your computer or scanner and an image-editing program. When using your computer, the pattern is printed out at the appropriate enlargement size. This method will generally require tiling standard-size printer paper. Another option is to use an opaque projector. Place your drawing under the unit and project a larger image of the pattern onto a piece of tracing paper or fabric taped to a wall. You can choose to simply go to the local copy center for enlargements, or you can forget technology altogether and use the old reliable grid method.

Because this pattern is fairly simple, let's leave technology aside. Here are instructions for using the grid method to enlarge the pattern for "Cloud Fly-By" on page 33. Follow the same instructions to enlarge any of the patterns in this book. This is a quick, simple, and technology-free way to enlarge a pattern and be on your way.

We'll enlarge the design to a working size of 18" x 22". You'll need a pencil, an 8½" x 11" piece of tracing paper, and an 18" x 22" piece of tracing paper.

1. Using a pencil, trace the pattern on page 33 directly onto the smaller piece of tracing paper.

2. Cut the pattern along the edges of the drawing.

3. Fold this paper in half, and then fold in half again.

Fold the traced pattern in half, and then fold in half again.

4. Turn the folded paper 90° without unfolding it. Repeat the folding in this direction. Unfold, and you will have a grid of rectangles as shown on page 24.

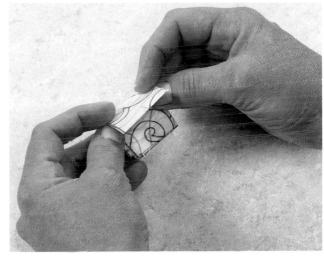

Fold the paper in half twice; turn it 90° and fold in half twice more to create a grid.

Unfold to create a grid of rectangles.

5. Repeat the folding process with the 18" x 22" piece of tracing paper. When unfolded, you will have a matching grid of proportional dimensions on both papers.

6. Look at one section of the smaller grid and note the lines of the pattern. Now draw what you see in the corresponding section of the larger grid. I suggest starting at the top left corner. When the first section is enlarged, go on to the next section, working left to right and top to bottom until everything is enlarged. Look at the entire pattern. If changes or corrections are needed, make them with pencil at this point.

Start in the upper left-hand corner and draw the portion of the image found within the same grid section of the smaller pattern.

7. After all the lines are successfully drawn onto the larger grid; go over each with a fine-point permanent marker.

Preparing the Fabric

After the tracing-paper pattern is complete, the fun begins. Remembering all the ideas about color, texture, and mood discussed on pages 17–20, select the two fabrics that will be used for the quilted background.

These fabrics provide high contrast and set the mood for an inspiring sunset.

1. Press your selected fabrics and cut an 18" x 22" piece from each.

2. Referring to "Top or Bottom" on page 25, decide which fabric will be on top and which one will be underneath. Lay the fabric that will be underneath out on a flat surface so that the wrong side is facing up.

3. Lay a piece of colored, wax-free transfer paper right-side down, and then lay the enlarged tracing paper pattern face down. Align the edges of the tracing paper with the fabric edges and place two or three pieces of masking tape along the top edge to keep everything aligned as you work.

Work from the Back

When working with the pattern, make sure that you turn it over and work from the back; otherwise the design will come out backward.

4. Using a blunt tool, (my favorite is a wooden knitting needle), go over each of the lines of the pattern, moving the transfer paper underneath as needed.

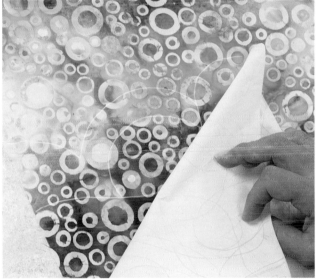

Use a blunt tool to trace the lines of the pattern and transfer it to the fabric.

5. Turn the marked fabric over so it's right-side up. Lay the second fabric on top, right-side up as well, and make sure the edges are aligned.

6. Tape the fabric layers down to the flat surface and pin them together with safety pins spaced about 4" to 5" apart.

Top or Bottom

The Fast-Piece Appliqué background technique requires that your two fabrics be layered, with one placed on the bottom and one on top prior to sewing them together. Here are some guidelines for deciding which fabric should be on top.

In most cases, place the fabric you wish to see more of, the dominant fabric, on top

If one of your fabrics is much darker than the other, place the darker fabric on top.

If you can see a pattern or color through the top fabric when layering them, reverse the order.

Sewing and Trimming the Quilt Top

Set your sewing machine for straight stitching with a neutral thread on the top and in the bobbin. Neutral thread could be beige, gray, or black. It should be visible, but not highly contrasting.

1. On the marked side of the pinned fabrics, stitch all the lines of the pattern. Remove the pins and press.

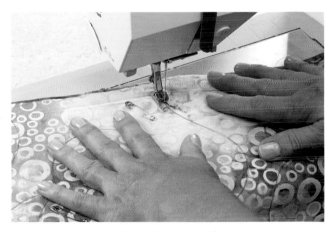

Sew along the marked lines.

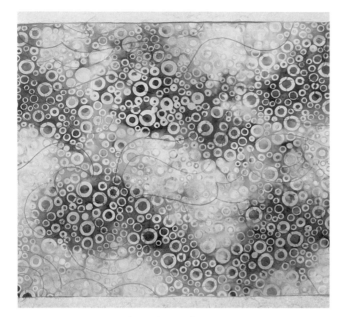

Stitch all the lines of the pattern.

Trim the top fabric as close to the stitching line as possible.

2. Use the trim diagram below and mark the individual sections to be removed with a chalkliner tool. You will trim either the black sections or white sections, depending on how you layered your fabrics.

Trim diagram

3. With duckbill appliqué scissors, carefully trim away the top fabrics from the marked sections getting as close to the sewing line as possible. *Note:* Trim only the top. Do not trim the fabric underneath.

Center Cut-Out Trick

When you begin the cutting-out process, trim the sections that are along an edge first. When you get to a center cut, try this little trick.

Use a long straight pin to grab a couple of threads of fabric from the center of a section that you're planning to cut. Once on the pin, use the duckbill appliqué scissors to snip the fabric right under the pin. This creates a hole that you can now fit your scissors safely into so that you can trim away the top fabric without cutting through the lower fabric.

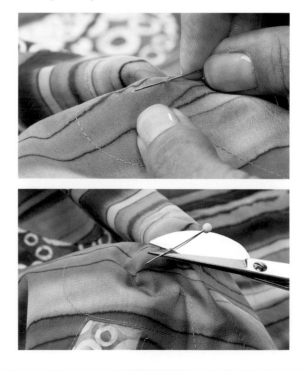

THE BASICS OF FAST-PIECE APPLIQUÉ BACKGROUNDS

4. After trimming, the top is complete. Press the piece and it's ready for couching and quilting. Use a little spray starch if desired.

COUCHING AND QUILTING BASICS

Couching and quilting create linear design elements. We stitch or couch lines in many ways and in many configurations to create detail, shape, or texture. For example, take a close look at the bark of a tree, or the fur on your cat. You'll begin to see some basic lines that will help you see that these things are three-dimensional, and they'll help you see the unique character and life of the living thing or object. Artists see and simplify these lines to bring dimension, character, and life to their work.

Take the Line Challenge

The next time you're walking around a gallery, looking up a favorite artist on the Internet, or even visiting the zoo, note how lines are used or not used. How does this affect what's presented?

I took these photos during a visit to the zoo. These are just a few examples of linear elements found there.

Texture and Definition with Lines

Shapes are naturally occurring design elements for quilters. Every time we take scissors to fabric, the outcome is a shape. I've always been drawn to the linear aspects that quilting and/or couching add. These processes provide contrast, patterning, and detail to the shapes in our quilts and create secondary patterns just waiting to be noticed and wondered over.

Whether stitched by hand or machine, couching and quilting are the ways I choose to represent linear elements in my quilt art. I often use repeating lines to outline and define shapes or create patterns that define depth and add texture and interest. I may add many details to make the patterns appear highly complex, or I may use simple variations that allow viewers the opportunity to fill in the details using their own imaginations. Following are four examples of ways to use linear designs in your quilts.

Use lines that echo the contours of a particular shape to define it and add dimension.

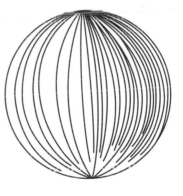

Vary the number and spacing of parallel lines together to show direction and shading.

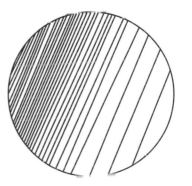

Use parallel wavy lines to create the appearance of grass, fur, or hair.

Produce the look of rippled water patterns or wood graining with undulating, echoing lines.

Remember that the appearance is also affected by what materials are used and how they're applied. Threads vary in weight and texture, and there's a huge selection of thread to choose from. With all these variables, there are nearly limitless possibilities!

The Right Tools for Couching and Quilting

Here are the items that you'll need from your sewing kit and tool bag in order to prepare the pressed background for couching and quilting.

Masking tape

Batting

Fabric for backing

Safety pins for basting

Decorative yarns

Decorative thread (top)

Bobbin thread (selected to work with the quilt back)

Couching or cording foot or open-toe foot

These are some of my favorite decorative threads; they add a bit of sparkle when used for couching over various yarns.

Preparing the Quilt Sandwich

1. Lay the ironed backing fabric right side down on your cutting mat and use masking tape to secure it in place.

2. Center the batting and quilt top on the backing fabric, right side up, and tape in place.

3. Secure the layers using safety pins every few inches.

Couching

You'll be couching yarn along all the raw edges of your quilt design to cover up the stitching lines and to delineate the shapes. Be sure to read "Tips for Successful Couching" on page 29 before you begin.

1. Select yarns for couching that coordinate with the fabrics in your quilt top.

2. Thread your machine with a decorative thread on the top. Choose a metallic, rayon, cotton blend, or other synthetic thread that will work with the yarns you're planning to use. Use a bobbin thread that is compatible with the top thread and the back of the quilt, as the bobbin thread will show on the back of the quilt.

3. Feed the selected yarn through foot opening. If you're using an open-toe foot, hold the yarn in place below the opening.

4. Set your machine for a zigzag stitch. Set the stitch length to 0 and the width to 3 mm or 3.5 mm.

5. Start at a seam along the outer edge and take about four or five stitches in place to lock the stitch.

6. Reset the stitch length to 3 mm or 3.5 mm. Resume stitching, couching the yarn over the seam line so that it covers the stitching and the raw edge of the fabric. Remove any safety pins that are in the way as you go.

7. At the end of the seam, stop and reset the stitch length to 0; again take four or five stitches in place to lock the thread and trim excess thread at the locked stitch.

8. Continue couching over all the raw edges, taking the safety pins out as you go.

9. When all the couching is done, remove the remaining pins and press the quilt from the back.

Tips for Successful Couching

- Whenever possible, begin couching with a line that starts at one quilt edge and goes through the center of the quilt to the opposite edge. Then work from that line toward the outside edges. If there's no stitching line running completely across the quilt, begin at a point near the center and work out toward the edges of the quilt.

- Practice couching on a sample quilt sandwich first to check stitch quality and tension. This is especially helpful when trying a new yarn or thread for the first time. Stitch at least 3" on your sample and check the stitching on both the front and the back. If the bobbin thread is showing on the front, loosen the tension (to a lower number). If the top thread is showing on the back, increase the tension (to a higher number).

- Let the sewing machine stitch at its own pace; don't force the fabric through.

- If the yarn and stitching begin to bunch or tighten, increase the *length* (not the width) of the zigzag stitch.

- If the stitching does not cover the width of the yarn (from side to side), increase the *width* of your zigzag stitch.

- When stitching a tight turn, lower the needle on the inside of the turn and keep it in the lowered position while adjusting the quilt. If it's a very tight turn, take a second stitch in place at the turning point before continuing.

Quilting

The couching serves as quilting to hold the layers together, and once it's complete you can add additional quilting, if desired. When deciding on the quilting design, keep your theme in mind and consider the couching lines. You may decide to use general continuous-line patterns that echo the couching.

Once you have a general idea of how you want to quilt an area, I recommend that you sketch the pattern on paper to get an idea of size and spacing and to help determine how to move the quilt under the needle. Drawing the design also creates a memory connection between your hand and your mind so that when you begin to machine quilt, your hand knows the motion required to create the quilting pattern. It also helps to hang the practice drawing above your sewing machine as a guide.

Following the basic sketch, use a chalk-liner tool to block out an area where you want a specific pattern. The chalk liner lets you easily mark the quilt and stand back to view the general placement before making the final decision of where to place your quilting. The chalk remains visible while working on the quilting, but is easily dusted off when done.

BASIC BINDING

After your quilt is couched and quilted, it's time to bind the edges.

1. Square up the quilt.

2. Cut 2"-wide straight-grain strips (selvage to selvage) from the binding fabric. You will need enough strips to go around the quilt plus approximately 10" additional for joining strips and mitering corners.

3. With right sides together, join the strips end to end to make one long strip.

4. Trim one end of the strip at a 45° angle and press the raw angled end under ¼". This will be the beginning of the binding strip.

5. Fold the binding strip in half lengthwise, wrong sides together, and press. Your strip should now be 1" wide.

6. Starting in the middle of one side of the layered quilt, position the binding strip along the edge of the quilt top, raw edges aligned. Using a ¼" seam allowance, stitch the binding to the quilt, beginning several inches from the angled end. Stop sewing ¼" from the first corner; backstitch. Cut the threads and remove the quilt from the machine.

7. Rotate the quilt so you're ready to sew the next edge. Fold the binding up at a 90° angle so the fold makes a 45° angle. Fold the binding back down onto itself so the raw edges are aligned. Begin stitching at the fold and continue until you're ¼" from the next corner; backstitch. Repeat the folding and stitching process at each corner.

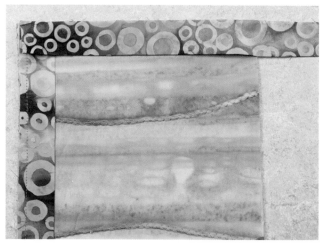

Fold the binding strip up and then down so the fold makes a 45° angle.

Fold the binding back down onto itself, aligning the binding and quilt raw edges.

8. When you're close to the beginning of the binding, trim the end of the strip so it overlaps the beginning by approximately 1". Continue sewing the binding in place.

9. Before sewing the binding to the back by hand, add any desired dimensional stitching, beading or other embellishment.

10. Fold the binding to the back of the quilt and hand blindstitch the folded edge in place, covering the machine stitching.

When to Bead and Embellish

I found out early on that once you add beads to a quilt, it's difficult to machine stitch binding strips to the outside edge. I suggest that you attach the binding to your quilt, and then add any beads. Lastly, after finishing your embellishment, turn the binding to the back and hand stitch it in place.

FACED BINDING

Faced binding gives you a lovely finished edge with no binding fabric showing on the front of the finished quilt. Because the strips are cut wider, allow more fabric, about twice as much as for basic binding.

1. Square up the quilt.

2. Cut 4½"-wide straight-grain strips (selvage to selvage) from the binding fabric. You'll need four strips, one for each edge of the quilt. Add 2" to the length of each side of the quilt and cut the binding strips to that length. (Join strips end to end with right sides together if needed to get the length needed for sides that are longer than 40".)

3. Fold the binding strips in half lengthwise with wrong sides together and press, creating four strips, each 2¼" wide.

4. With right sides together and raw edges aligned, place and pin a binding strip along the top edge of the quilt, leaving about 1" extending beyond each corner.

5. With a neutral-color thread in the sewing machine, begin sewing ¼" from the corner, backstitch, and then stitch using a ¼" seam allowance. Sew until you are ¼" from the next corner and backstitch.

6. Repeat step 5 along the bottom edge of the quilt, and then press the binding and seam allowances outward so they lie flat.

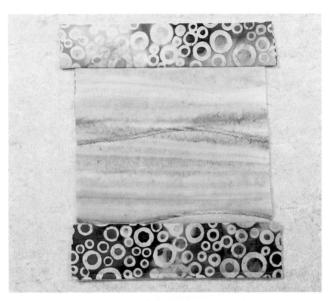

Sew the binding to opposite sides of the quilt, starting and stopping ¼" away from the corners.

7. Sew binding to the remaining two sides of the quilt; press.

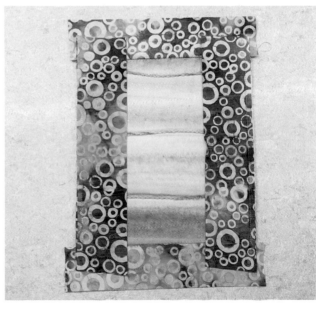

Stitch the remaining two binding strips to the quilt and press.

8. After all the sides are sewn and pressed, snip a small triangle of batting, backing, and quilt top off each corner to reduce bulk.

9. Add any desired dimensional stitching and beading.

10. To turn the binding to the back, start at the top edge and fold the attached binding fabric toward the back of the quilt. Iron, trim the excess binding along the sides, and pin in place.

11. Stitch this length of the binding in place by hand. Repeat along the bottom edge. Press the binding from the back of the quilt.

12. Trim excess fabric from the side binding strips so that you have ¼" extending beyond the sides. Fold the binding to the back of quilt on each side. Iron, and pin in place.

13. Turn the ¼" of fabric under at each corner and tuck it in so that the edge is even with the previously sewn edge; pin in place.

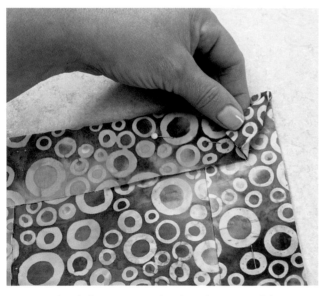

Turn back the corner and tuck in the excess fabric.

14. Repeat to turn under the binding fabric at all corners and hand sew the remaining binding to the backing.

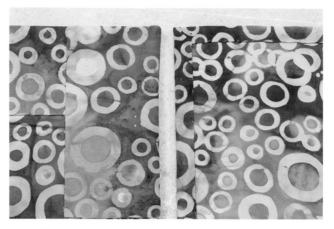

Faced binding is on the left and basic binding is on the right.

TIME TO EMBELLISH

With the background quilt stitched and ready, it's time to create the star elements for our quilts. Each of the projects that follow will provide you with directions for creating your own unique embellishments. All have been selected not only for the fun, whimsical opportunities they provide, but also for their compatibility for use on a quilt. It's time to jump in, play, and have fun while adding new tools and methods to your "Bag of Tools!"

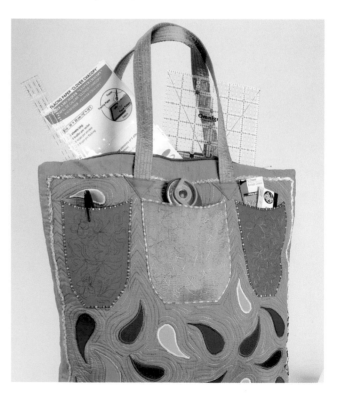

Enlarge pattern 250%.

THE TRUTH ABOUT CATS AND DOGS
quilted embellishments

Cats and dogs are at their lovable best when they're in their favorite place. For the cat, it's lounging on the wonderful soft rug in the sun after capturing his favorite toy. The dog is happiest while running down the path at the park. The animals for each of these quilts are created separately; then each becomes the star of his favorite spot once appliquéd to the background quilt.

Finished size: 21½" x 21½"

TURNED-FABRIC EMBELLISHMENTS

Both the cat and the dog are separate small quilted creatures made from fabric and batting scraps. The fronts are quickly assembled using my Fast-Piece Appliqué technique; then they are layered, stitched, turned, embellished, and attached. The final bling for the little dog's collar seemed perfect, and my cats really love going after these feathery, flying toys. I found these items while strolling happily down the aisles of my local pet store.

From Your Bag of Tools

Some of the special tools you'll want to grab out of your bag of tools are ones that will help you turn the pieces right side out. These may include a hemostat, knitting needles, small crochet hook, or crewel needle (something small enough to get into some tight corners, with a slightly blunt point).

MATERIALS FOR BACKGROUND QUILT

Cat

1 yard of large-scale red print

1 yard of medium-scale red print

Dog

1 yard of large-scale brown-and-green print

1 yard of medium-scale brown print

Cat or Dog

¼ yard of fabric for basic binding

1 yard of fabric for backing

26" x 26" piece of batting

Yarn for couching

MATERIALS FOR EMBELLISHMENTS

Cat

1 fat quarter of black velveteen fabric

1 fat quarter of black silk/cotton blend fabric

1 fat eighth of white silk/cotton blend fabric

Scraps of green or yellow cotton fabric

1 fat quarter of black cotton fabric for backing

18" x 20" piece of batting

Freezer paper

Buttons or beads for eyes

Dog

1 fat quarter of white velveteen fabric

1 fat eighth of white silk/cotton blend fabric

1 fat quarter of white cotton fabric for backing

6" x 12" piece of black velveteen fabric

Scraps of pink cotton fabric

12" x 20" piece of batting

Buttons for eyes

CUTTING

From *each* of the two background fabrics, cut:

1 square, 22" x 22"

STITCHING THE BACKGROUND QUILT

Enlarge the background pattern for the cat (page 39) or the dog (page 40) and draw it to full size, 22" x 22". Follow the steps in "Cloud Fly-By" on page 22 to enlarge the pattern, prepare the fabric, and complete the construction of the quilt top. Use the appropriate trim diagram below when cutting away the pattern sections to prepare for couching. Refer to "Couching and Quilting Basics" on page 27 to complete the background quilt and apply basic binding.

Trim diagram for cat quilt

Trim diagram for dog quilt

PREPARING THE PATTERN AND FABRICS

Now, the embellishment fun begins! The step-by-step instructions here are for preparing the cat. Follow the same basic steps for the dog (see "Working with Velveteen Fabric" on page 62).

1. Enlarge the patterns for the cat or the dog (page 41). Note that each pattern is made of two sections, the head and the body.

2. Place freezer paper, shiny side down, over the enlarged paper pattern sections and trace the pattern using a permanent marker. Add the pattern

numbers and draw hash marks across the lines of the pattern.

3. Cut the freezer-paper template apart by cutting directly on the lines.

4. Iron the freezer-paper templates (shiny side down) to the right side of the chosen fabrics. Use the chart below for reference.

5. Cut each piece from the fabric, leaving ½" extra around the entire template.

Iron the templates to the fabrics and cut ½" outside the template.

Fabrics for Cat	Pattern Pieces
Black velveteen	Head 1, Body 3
Black silk/cotton blend	Head 5, Body 1
White silk/cotton blend	Head 4, Body 2
Green or yellow cotton	Head 2, 3
Fabrics for Dog	**Pattern Pieces**
White velveteen	Head 1, 5; Body 2
White silk/cotton blend	Body 3
Black velveteen	Head 4, Body 1
Pink cotton	Head 2, 3, 6

STITCHING THE EMBELLISHMENT

Set your sewing machine for straight stitching. Use a neutral thread (beige, gray, or black) on the top and in the bobbin. It should be visible but not highly contrasting.

1. Select the prepared pattern and fabric for pieces 1 and 2 for the head of the cat and place them together side-by-side on an ironing board.

2. Butt the lines on the templates together, matching the hash marks on the templates. Once lined up, lift up the edge of the freezer paper on one of the pieces and slide one fabric piece over the other, leaving only the width of a sewing machine needle between the edges of the two templates. Iron the freezer-paper template that was lifted back into place.

3. Straight stitch between the two freezer-paper templates.

Sew in the space between the templates.

Lights and Darks

When joining a very light fabric to a dark one, lift the freezer-paper template from the light fabric and slide the dark fabric on top to sew. This will eliminate any shadows that might be seen through the light fabric.

4. After sewing the two pieces together, lift up the edge of the freezer-paper template, exposing the sewing line and the raw edge of the fabric on top. Lift only enough to trim the excess. Trim the raw edge as close to the sewing line as possible using duckbill appliqué scissors. *Note:* Trim only the top. Do not trim the back. After trimming, iron the freezer paper back into place.

5. Add fabric piece 3 and trim.

Lift the edge of the freezer paper and trim the excess fabric along the edge of the stitching.

6. Sew piece 4 to piece 5, and then sew that section to section 1/2/3 to create the head. Trim after each addition. The paper templates can be removed as you finish stitching next to them. For the cat body, sew pieces 1 and 2 together, and then add 3.

7. Remove the paper templates carefully and set them aside. Press the sewn cat sections.

8. Press the freezer-paper templates (body and head separately) onto the wrong side of the black backing fabric.

9. Lay out the batting for the cat and lay the sewn cat sections face up on top of it.

10. Lay the backing fabric on top of the sewn cat section with the freezer-paper template face up. Insert pins through the top to the sewn cat to align the layers. Once lined up, pin layers together.

Insert pins to align the sewn cat with the template on top.

11. Set your sewing machine for a straight stitch and use neutral sewing thread in the top and bobbin. Stitch very close to the edge of the freezer paper, around the outside edge.

12. Trim excess fabric, leaving approximately 1/16" seam allowance. Clip curves and cut a slit in the backing fabric so you can turn the pieces right-side out using the turning tools you have on hand. Press the head and body from the wrong side.

13. Couch the seams and embellish your cat as desired. Then hand appliqué it to your quilted background (body first). Position it as you like. I left part of the cat hanging off the edge for interest.

FINISHING THE QUILT

1. Add any beading or embellishing stitches to the background.

2. Hand stitch the binding in place.

Adding to Your Bag of Tools

After making the dog or cat, you can create all sorts of dimensional embellishments. Use fast-piece appliqué, layer, stitch, and turn. Couch and embellish to your heart's content and appliqué to your quilt. You can never have too many options in your bag of tools!

Background pattern for cat quilt
Enlarge 400%.

Background pattern for dog quilt
Enlarge 400%.

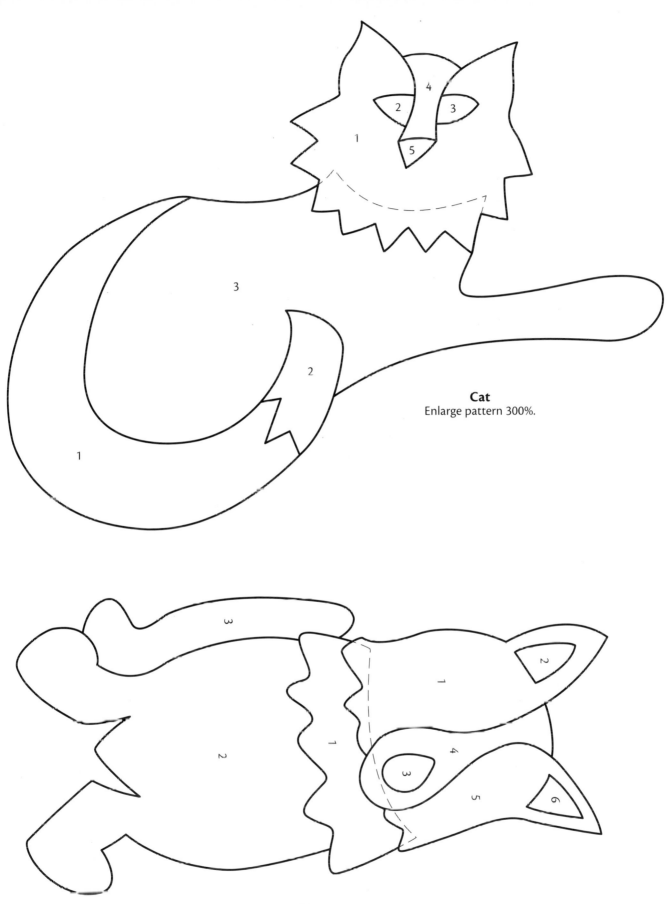

Cat
Enlarge pattern 300%.

Dog
Enlarge pattern 300%.

DANCE THE NIGHT AWAY
couched fabric and air-dry clay beads

Imagine dancing the night away, barefoot, under a full moon. The background for this escapade has us dancing among the rolling hills. The dancers are fabric embellishments that are added after the background quilt is done, and then couched into place. Adorn the dancers further with wild masks made out of air-dry clay.

Finished size: 32" x 24"

FUN FABRICATING WITH FABRIC AND CLAY

For this quilt there are two types of embellishments the fabric dancers and their special face masks. The couched fabric jewels dance their way across the finished quilt background. Since they're made out of fabric, they remain flexible and offer the endless possibilities that fabric itself offers. Color, texture, and linear movement can all be part of the special fabrics you select for the dancers. Air-dry clay is used to create the masks for each of the dancers. This material is easy to use and readily available. You can easily create special beads with simple tools and a rubber stamp or two. These beads are so much fun to make and they're super easy.

MATERIALS FOR BACKGROUND QUILT

1 yard of multicolored blue fabric

1 yard of multicolored blue green fabric

½ yard of fabric for faced binding

1 yard of fabric for backing

36" x 28" piece of batting

Yarn for couching

MATERIALS FOR EMBELLISHMENTS

Couched Fabric Dancers

½ yard of light, large-scale print

½ yard of a lightweight cotton or cotton-blend batting

Freezer paper

Yarn for couching around the dancers

Beads

1 package of air-dry clay*

Plastic knife

1 plastic resealable bag, 1-quart size

1 set of bead-making tools, an awl, or a very narrow straw

Rubber stamp or push mold**

Cornstarch (for push molds)

Narrow nail file sticks or fine sandpaper

Acrylic paint

Small paintbrush

Matte or gloss medium, such as Liquitex

Embroidery floss for attaching bead masks

*I use Prang DAS Air-Hardening Modeling Clay, available from art-supply stores. The smallest package is 1.1 pounds, which is plenty.

**There are a lot of rubber-stamp or push-mold options available, but you may also create your own. I often make my own rubber-stamp designs as for this quilt by carving them out of Speedy-Cut Speedball Rubber. The photographs beginning on page 45 show a push mold being used to make a clay bead suitable for a dancer's mask.

CUTTING

From *each* of the background fabrics, cut:

1 piece, 32½" x 24½"

STITCHING THE BACKGROUND QUILT

Enlarge the background pattern (page 47) and draw it to full size, 32½" x 24½". Follow the steps in "Cloud Fly-By" on page 22 to enlarge the pattern, prepare the fabric, and complete the construction of the quilt top. Use the trim diagram below when cutting away the pattern sections to prepare for couching. Refer to "Couching and Quilting Basics" on page 27 to complete the background quilt and apply faced binding.

Trim diagram

MAKING AND ATTACHING THE DANCERS

1. Enlarge the patterns for the three dancers (page 47) and trace them onto freezer paper.

2. Cut the freezer-paper templates out along the drawn lines and iron each template to the right side of the selected fabrics. Loosely cut around the template.

3. Lay the dancers onto the batting and loosely cut around the fabric.

4. Place each of the dancers, layered with the batting, onto the quilt where desired and pin in place. Note that a small quilt sandwich is shown in the photos, rather than the actual quilt background.

Pin the layered template, fabric, and batting to the quilt.

5. Using a straight stitch, sew around the dancer, just along the edge of the freezer-paper template.

Stitch the layered embellishment
along the outside edge of the template.

6. Remove the pins and freezer paper. Trim the excess fabric and batting as close to the stitching line as possible.

Trim the excess fabric and batting.

7. Couch yarns over the raw edges, referring to "Couching and Quilting Basics" on page 27 as needed.

Materials for air-dry clay beads

FABRICATING THE DANCERS' MASKS

1. On a clean, flat work surface, open the package of clay and slice off approximately 2" of the clay material. Place the remaining clay into the plastic resealable bag; otherwise, it will dry out.

2. Cut the slice into three approximately equal parts, and roll each part into a smooth ball. The balls make it easy to push consistent amounts into the rubber stamp or mold.

Roll the clay into balls to be used with the rubber stamp or mold.

3. Lay the rubber stamp or push mold on your work table, face up. If you use a push mold, rub a small amount of cornstarch over the surface area before placing the clay in the mold to prevent sticking. Carefully push one of the clay balls into the design. Once a desired thickness of approximately ¼" is reached, pull the stamp or mold away from the clay; try not to pull the clay as that may distort the shape.

referring to "Couching and Quilting Basics" on page 27

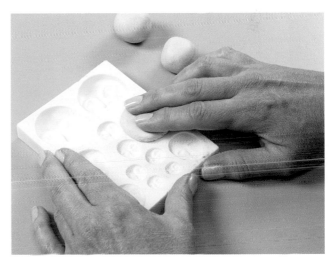

Push the clay ball into the mold.

4. Carefully push a bead-making tool, an awl, or a narrow straw through the clay to make the hole or holes needed to attach the mask to the quilt.

Make holes in the clay so that it can be attached easily to the quilt.

Tips for Working with Clay

- Be sure to place any clay not being used back inside the plastic resealable bag.
- Add small amounts of water if needed to make the clay more pliable.
- If you aren't happy with a design, you can rework the clay by rerolling it into a ball until it's smooth again.
- Once dry, any slight imperfections in the clay can be sanded away.

5. Set the pieces out to dry overnight. If you're too impatient, as I am sometimes, you can place the molded pieces on a cookie sheet covered with aluminum foil and dry them in the oven. I preheat the oven to 325° and leave them in for 20 minutes. Then I remove the tray, turn the pieces over, and place it back in the oven for another 20 minutes. Be sure to follow the manufacturer's instructions for drying.

6. Once the beads are dry, sand and paint them as desired. Seal them with a final coat of gloss or matte medium. After the paint and sealer has dried, stitch the beads in place as you would any other large bead. I used six strands of embroidery floss to attach them to the quilt.

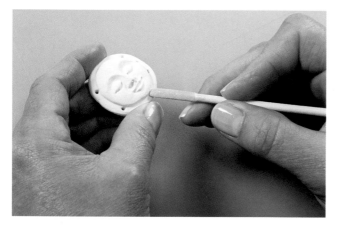

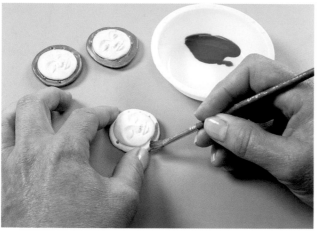

FINISHING THE QUILT

1. With the dancers in place, all having a good time, add any further stitching and beading.

2. Hand stitch the binding in place as described on page 31.

Beautiful Beads

Some of my favorite tools for sanding and fine touches are found at the beauty-supply store. You'll find these nail file sticks with nail files and other similar items. These thin pencil-like tools have varying-weight sandpaper built into the tips and make it easy to clean up any little blemishes on the beads before painting them.

Adding to Your Bag of Tools

Using fabric as an embellishment really has a long history. When you add batting, it gives the fabric embellishment more presence. In this quilt, it allows the dancers to take center stage to show off their masks. With air-dry clay, the possibilities for making fun and original beads and other embellishments are endless. You now have two fabulous new techniques to add to your bag of tools.

Background and Dancers patterns
Enlarge 333%.

STARRY NIGHT
fused fabric and angelina fibers

There's nothing like a romantic evening walk under a star-filled sky. Many of us live in urban areas that block out many of the stars from our nightly viewing; but this just makes it all the more entrancing when we find ourselves under a clear, unending starlit sky. Add a full moon, and the setting is complete. This quilt is made in memory of many a nighttime walk under skies lit up and twinkling, inviting fantasy and reflection. It also reflects my hope to enjoy many more such beautiful evenings. Fabrics of different types are used in this project to add a sense of magic and mystery that's always present on just such a nighttime walk. Then special beads and buttons are placed to give it even more sparkle.

Finished size: 24" x 32"

STICKY, FUSIBLE, AND FUN EMBELLISHMENTS

There are many fusible products that we can use to create unique, personal fabrics to get just the right effect for a particular quilt. I refer to these as the sticky products; the various types of glues make them simple to use. In this project, we'll use two sticky products along with various fabrics to build our featured embellishments. The products that will help us create the dark, silhouetted trees and the silvery moon are fusible web and bondable Angelina fibers.

MATERIALS FOR BACKGROUND QUILT

1 yard of purple, gray, and black striped batik

1 yard of purple, gray, and black print

½ yard of fabric for basic binding

1 yard of fabric for backing

26" x 34" piece of batting

Yarn for couching

MATERIALS FOR EMBELLISHMENTS
Moon

1 fat eighth of white velveteen fabric

9" x 21" piece of lightweight cotton or cotton-blend batting

Freezer paper

1 ½-ounce package of bondable Angelina fibers

Pressing sheets (2 are needed)*

Yarn for couching

Trees

1 fat quarter of black on black print for tree

1 fat quarter of black cotton/silk blend fabric for tree

1 fat quarter of black fabric for tree backing

½ yard of mediumweight fusible web (18" wide)

Freezer paper

Decorative threads

*Parchment paper can substitute for the pressing sheets.

Samples of the many colors of Angelina fibers available

CUTTING

From *each* of the two background fabrics, cut:

1 piece, 24½" x 32½"

STITCHING THE BACKGROUND QUILT

Enlarge the background pattern (page 52) and draw it to full size, 24½" x 32½". Follow the steps in "Cloud Fly-By" on page 22 to enlarge the pattern, prepare the fabric, and complete the construction of the quilt top. Use the trim diagram below when cutting away the pattern sections to prepare for couching. Refer to "Couching and Quilting Basics" on page 27 to complete the background quilt and apply basic binding.

Trim diagram

MAKING THE MOON

1. Enlarge the moon and outer ring patterns (page 52) and trace them onto freezer paper.

2. Cut out the moon freezer-paper template along the drawn lines and iron it to the right side of the white velveteen. Loosely cut around the template.

3. Lay the moon on the batting and loosely cut around the fabric.

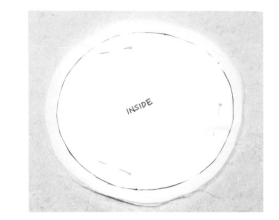

Cut the moon from white velveteen and layer it with batting.

4. The outer ring will be made of "fabric" created from the Angelina fibers. Lay the outer-ring pattern on your ironing board and place the pressing sheet on top. Using small wisps of Angelina fibers, slowly build up the layers of fibers by laying them over the pattern. You can leave the center open, like a donut, since the moon will cover this area. Continue adding fibers until there is little open space between the fibers. (*Note*: If you're using two or more colors of the fibers, you can mix them as desired at this point.)

Using small wisps of Angelina fibers, build up the layers that will become the outer ring of the moon.

5. When the fibers are as dense as desired, lay another pressing sheet over the fibers. Press the sheet lightly with an iron, following the manufacturer's instructions, to bond and create the fabric. Allow to cool.

6. Position the fiber fabric on the quilt top. Center the batting and the velveteen moon (with the pattern pressed in place), over the fiber fabric. Pin in place.

7. With your sewing machine, sew a straight stitch just around the outside edge of the center moon pattern.

Pin the Angelina fibers and moon in position and stitch in place.

8. Remove the freezer-paper template; trim the excess batting and velveteen close to the stitching line with duckbill appliqué scissors.

9. Couch yarn around the raw edges of the moon.

MAKING THE TREES

1. Enlarge the tree patterns on page 53 and trace them onto freezer paper.

2. Press the black backing fabric on your ironing board. Press the fusible web to the wrong side of the fabric and let cool; then remove the paper from the fusible web.

3. Press the wrong side of the black print and black cotton/silk blend fabrics to the adhesive side of the black backing fabric.

4. Place the freezer-paper templates on the right side of the prepared fabrics and press in place.

Adding to Your Bag of Tools

Using fusible products to create unique fabrics is only one of many ways they may be used on our quilts. Since fusibles are readily available and easy to work with, I hope that you'll put them in your bag of tools and pull them out regularly.

5. Cut the trees from their respective fabrics on the drawn line, and then remove the paper template.

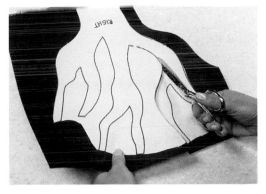

Press the freezer-paper templates to the prepared fabrics and cut out the tree shapes.

6. Referring to the photograph on page 49 for placement guidance, position the left tree on the quilt background and tape in place. Using masking tape, rather than pins, to hold the fused fabrics in place keeps everything flat and in position without creating bulk or bunching.

7. Set your sewing machine for a straight stitch and stitch the left tree to the quilt, sewing close to the edges of the tree. Remove the tape just before stitching over it. *Note:* When selecting thread to stitch the fused elements in place, remember that the bobbin thread will be visible on the back of your quilt.

8. Repeat steps 6 and 7 to stitch the right tree in place.

9. Quilt and embellish the trees as desired.

FINISHING THE QUILT

1. With the featured fusible elements stitched in place, add any additional quilting, dimensional stitching, or beading.

2. Hand stitch the binding in place as described on page 30.

Background, Moon, and Ring patterns
Enlarge 333%.

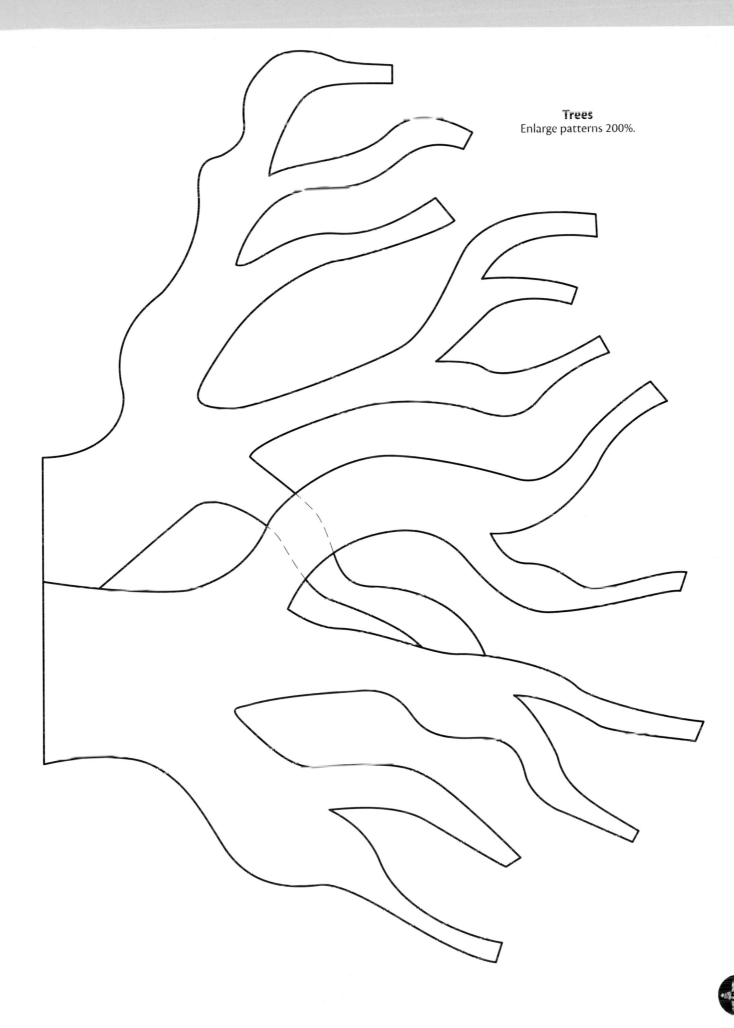

Trees
Enlarge patterns 200%.

WILD GARDEN PARTY
dimensional yarn embellishments

Think about it—wildflowers blowing in the wind, so tall that the sky is all you can see behind them. Nothing is prettier. Both my sisters have incredible gardens, each different, and in each you'll find beautiful, fanciful flowers. This quilt reminds me of all my favorite gardens, both wild and cultivated. The yarn embellishments add an unexpected, three-dimensional visual treat. The only missing elements are the wonderful scents of flowers in the sun. These yarn embellishments are an easy and fun way to add color and texture to a quilt.

Finished size: 32" x 24"

YARN EMBELLISHMENTS

With this technique, we'll fabricate wonderful flowers using the fusing methods learned in the last project and add yarn to create perky flower centers, garden fronds, and tight blossoms. We'll create the flowers by fusing layered fabrics and a layer of Angelina fibers. To this we'll add even more special embellishment elements using yarns and chenille stems, also known as pipe cleaners. These pliable embellishments can be bent to take on a variety of shapes and used in numerous ways. Best of all, they take on the color and texture of whatever yarns tickle our fancy.

MATERIALS FOR BACKGROUND QUILT

1 yard of small-scale sky blue fabric

1 yard of multicolored sky blue fabric

½ yard of fabric for faced binding

1 yard of fabric for backing

34" x 26" piece of batting

Yarn for couching

MATERIALS FOR EMBELLISHMENTS

Flowers and stems

1 fat eighth *each* of yellow and yellow orange silk fabric

1 fat quarter of golden yellow cotton fabric

1 fat eighth of medium green silk fabric

1 fat eighth of medium green cotton fabric

½ yard of mediumweight fusible web

Freezer paper

½-ounce package of bondable shiny blue green Angelina fibers

2 Pressing sheets

Dimensional yarn embellishments

14 chenille stems, 12" long (6 red and 8 green)*

Green and red yarns of various weights and textures

Tacky glue

Extra-fine patchwork pins

*These are also known as pipe cleaners.

CUTTING

From *each* of the sky blue fabrics, cut:
1 piece, 32½" x 24½"

STITCHING THE BACKGROUND QUILT

Enlarge the background pattern (page 59) and draw it to full size, 32½" x 24½". Follow the steps in "Cloud Fly-By" on page 22 to enlarge the pattern,

prepare the fabric, and complete the construction of the quilt top. Use the trim diagram below when cutting away the pattern sections to prepare for couching. Refer to "Couching and Quilting Basics" on page 27 to complete the background quilt and apply faced binding.

Trim diagram

FLOWERS AND STEMS

1. Enlarge the patterns on page 59 for the flowers, flower centers, and stems. Trace them onto freezer paper and cut on the drawn lines.

2. Follow steps 2–5 from "Making the Trees" on page 51 to create fused fabrics for the flowers, layering the yellow and yellow orange silk fabrics with the golden yellow cotton fabric. Prepare the fused fabric for the flower stems in the same manner using the green silk fabric layered with the green cotton fabric.

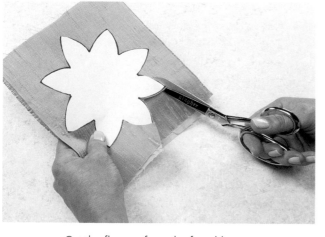

Cut the flowers from the fused layers of silk and cotton fabrics.

3. Quilt the flowers by hand or machine, if desired, to add decorative stitching and embellishing.

4. Make the five flower centers using the Angelina fibers, following the instructions in steps 4 and 5 from "Making the Moon" on page 50. Make a solid circle of Angelina fibers using the template for the flower centers.

5. Using the photograph on page 55 as a guide for placement, position the stems in place with masking tape and stitch them by machine. The masking tape holds the fused fabric in place without bulk or bunching. Just remember not to stitch over the tape.

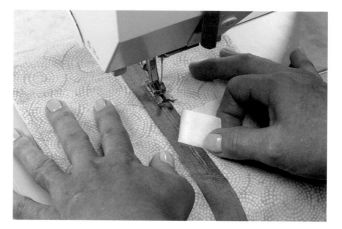

Stitch the stems to the background quilt as close to the edge as possible.

6. Place a flower at the top of each stem and add the Angelina fiber center. Pin and stitch around the edges of the Angelina flower centers, leaving the petals loose for dimension and allowing them to "blow in the wind."

CREATING YARN EMBELLISHMENTS

Use the green chenille stems for the stems and the red chenille stems for the flower centers and spiraled buds.

1. Insert one end of the chenille stem into the tacky glue until there's about ½" of glue at the end.

Dip one end of the chenille stem into tacky glue.

2. Tap off excess glue and place the end of the yarn so that about ½" is in the glue on the stem. Arrange the yarn strand so that it's perpendicular to the stem, in preparation for wrapping.

Place the end of the yarn in the glue and hold the yarn perpendicular to the stem.

3. Carefully begin wrapping the stem with yarn. Spin, twirl, and wrap, completely covering the chenille stem until you're about 1" from the other end.

Carefully wrap the stem with the yarn.

4. Insert the end of the stem into the tacky glue until there's about ½" of glue, and tap off the excess.

Dip the stem into the glue and tap off excess.

5. Continue wrapping the yarn along this end to finish. Cut the yarn and tuck the end in, securing it with glue.

Finish wrapping the final end.

6. Repeat to wrap each of the stems. You'll have a total of 14 wrapped pieces.

7. Bend each of the wrapped stems as desired. I used eight of the stems for stems or sprouts and created flat spirals for the flower centers.

Make flat spirals for the flower centers.

I wrapped some of the other stems around a pencil or dowel to make spring-like dimensional spirals to add to the emerging sprouts.

Make dimensional spirals to mimic flower buds.

8. Lay the wrapped stems on the quilted background and pin in place using extra-fine patchwork pins. Use a strong thread, such as beading thread, in a color that matches the wrapped stem. Sew them to the quilt by hand to attach them.

Hints for Stitching Wrapped Stems

● Use patchwork pins or quilting pins when pinning the wrapped stems; they make pinning easier.

● When hand sewing the stems in place, stitch along the sides, alternating sides and stitching over the stem every few stitches.

● To stitch the dimensional spiral, stitch along the lower stem first. When you reach the spiral, tack each spiral as you come to it.

FINISHING THE QUILT

1. With the wrapped yarn stems attached to the quilt background, add any beading or other embellishing to the background.

2. Hand stitch the binding in place as shown on page 31.

Adding to Your Bag of Tools

Now that you've added yarn and chenille stem embellishments to your repertoire, I encourage you to play—have fun mixing and matching and creating your own unique wildflowers, or coming up with other fun uses for these special fabricated yarn and chenille-stem embellishments. There's always room for more in your bag of tools!

Background and Flower patterns
Enlarge 333%.

WILDFLOWER WALK
wool-felt shapes and wool-roving gems

There's nothing better than a springtime walk through the hills near my home in order to see the wildflowers up close. As I walk along foot-worn paths, the flowers can be as tall as me. I chose very special fabrics in the gorgeous spring-green color that I love to build the background quilt for these flowers. I used velveteen to help express the softness of new grass, just sprouting. This combination of color and texture creates the perfect environment for some of my favorite embellishments. The featured embellishments in this project are made from wool felt and wool roving—the perfect fun and easy medium for a fiber junkie. Enjoy!

Finished size: 23½" x 31½"

WOOL EMBELLISHMENTS

Wool is the star in these techniques. The flowers are made of wool felt and the flower centers are made of felted wool roving. Roving is simply a bundle of wool fibers before they've been felted or spun into yarn. Felting is a process that turns raw wool fiber into a matted wool fabric we call felt. When exposed to moisture, heat, and pressure, microscopic scales in the raw wool open up. When the scales open and come into contact with other wool scales, they slide together and "lock" or mat. When the wool dries, the scales close in the locked position and create the wool felt.

The wool flowers are soft and dimensional, and the wool-roving gems add character and sparkle. Each wool gem can be beaded as desired. With a few simple supplies, you'll have a great time fabricating and using these felt shapes and little wool bundles on many projects.

MATERIALS FOR BACKGROUND QUILT

1 yard of spring green 100% cotton velveteen fabric

1 yard of tone-on-tone spring green print

½ yard of fabric for faced binding

⅞ yard of fabric for backing

26" x 34" piece of batting

Yarn for couching

MATERIALS FOR EMBELLISHMENTS

Wool-felt flowers

16" x 24" piece of blue 100% wool felt

16" x 24" piece of green 100% wool felt

8" x 8" piece of purple 100% wool felt

Batting scraps

Freezer paper

Embroidery thread and hand-stitching supplies

Wool roving gems

1 ounce *each* of purple, blue, and green wool roving

½ ounce of gold wool roving (optional)

Batting scraps

2 nylon knee-high stockings

Washing machine for felting

Laundry soap

Beads and hand bead-stitching supplies

Trim diagram

Working with Velveteen Fabric

There are a few things to keep in mind when selecting and working with velveteen fabric. First off, make sure that you select 100% cotton velveteen. This is now available in an amazing array of colors. Be aware that there are some velveteen fabrics that have a nap like cotton velveteen but they're on a polyester backing. These do not iron well and are best avoided.

Secondly, velveteen has a bit of stretch. When machine stitching the two fabrics together, keep the velveteen layer on the bottom so that the velveteen is engaged with the feed dogs.

Lastly, because velveteen has a nap, be careful when removing any freezer paper that is used with it. If it does not come off easily in one direction, remove the paper by pulling from the opposite direction.

CUTTING

From *each* of the background fabrics, cut:
1 piece, 24" x 32"

STITCHING THE BACKGROUND QUILT

Enlarge the background pattern (page 66) and draw it to full size, 24" x 32". Follow the steps in "Cloud Fly-By" on page 22 to enlarge the pattern, prepare the fabric, and complete the construction of the quilt top. Use the trim diagram above right when cutting away the pattern sections to prepare for couching. Refer to "Couching and Quilting Basics" on page 27 to complete the background quilt and apply faced binding.

MAKING THE WOOL-FELT FLOWERS

1. Trace the flower pattern on page 65 onto freezer paper including the inner line. Cut the template out on the outer drawn line.

2. Layer the blue and green wool felt together, right sides facing out. Iron the freezer-paper flower template to the felt and cut out the felt in pairs. Cut five pairs. Then layer the green and purple felt and cut one pair.

Cut the flowers in pairs from the layered wool felt.

3. Trim the flower template along the inner line and use it on the batting scraps to cut a pair of batting pieces for each flower.

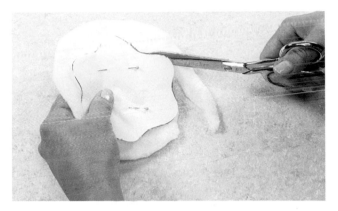

Cut two batting pieces for each flower.

4. Place two batting pieces between the two layers of wool felt for each flower cut previously. Pin the flower sandwiches together.

5. Thread a needle with embroidery floss. Use a running stitch, and stitch about ¼" from the outside edge of each flower. Stitch to embellish as desired. I used anywhere from two strands to five strands of floss in varying colors, some that coordinated with the wool colors and some that contrasted. I made several consecutive lines of stitching, echoing the first stitching until I was pleased with the look.

Stitch the wool-flower sandwich together with embroidery floss.

MAKING THE WOOL-ROVING GEMS

1. Using the pattern on page 65, make a paper template (any paper is fine) for the flower centers. Pin the paper template to three layers of batting scraps and cut a set of three circles of batting for each of the six wool gems you'll be making.

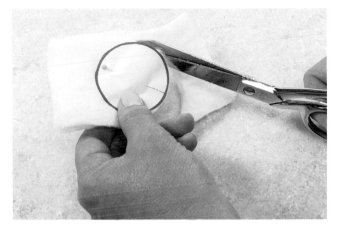

Pin the paper template to three layers of batting and cut the circles to create the stuffing for the wooly gems.

2. Pull a small wisp of purple (or main color) roving and spread it delicately out into a relatively flat layer. Repeat this three more times, laying each subsequent layer perpendicular to the one prior to it. (This layering will help bind all the fibers together when the felting takes place). You will have a total of four layers.

Layer small wisps of the roving, rotating each layer for good binding of the fibers.

3. Take small wisps of the highlight colors and add four layers in the same manner as in step 2. Add one more layer of the purple (or main color) roving.

Add various highlight colors to the layers of roving.

4. Lay a stack of three batting circles in the center of the layered roving and gently wrap the roving around them.

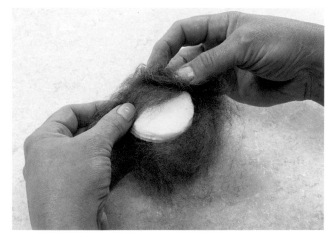

Wrap the layered roving around the batting circles.

5. Repeat steps 2 and 3; then place the wrapped batting from step 4 so that the loose ends face down into this new layered roving and gently wrap the batting once again.

6. Gently tuck the wisps of roving in around the wrapped batting in your palms. When it feels like it's beginning to loosely hold its shape, tie a knot near the end of a stocking and carefully place the roving bundle inside.

Place the roving bundle into the stocking.

7. Tie a knot on the other side of the bundle in the stocking to hold the roving package in place. Repeat the steps to make additional bundles and add them to the stockings. You will need a total of six wool gems.

Place the bundles of roving in the stocking and tie a knot between each one.

Felting and Beading

1. To felt the wrapped bundles, place them in your washing machine. Add hot soapy water and use high agitation to work the felting magic. Adding the stockings to a load of towels is perfect.

2. Remove the felted wool from the knotted stocking. Trim any stray fibers and allow to air dry.

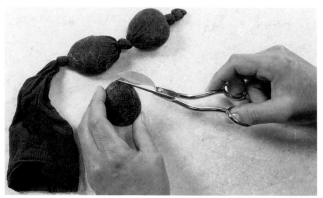

Remove the felted gems from the stocking and trim off any stray fibers.

3. Now you can have fun stitching and/or beading the gems to create the centers for the wildflowers on your quilt. Use a double-threaded needle and thread that matches the color of the wool.

Embellish each gem as desired, mixing and combining bead types and colors in any way that appeals to you.

PUTTING THE FELTED FLOWERS TOGETHER

1. After beading and stitching is complete, hand appliqué one wool gem to the center of each felt flower before you attach the flower to the quilt. Stitch along the outside, bottom edge of the wool gem, catching a small piece of the gem; then go through the felt flower.

2. Hand sew the completed wildflower embellishments to the quilted background. I gently fold the flowers back and stitch approximately 1" in from the outer edge of the flower. This leaves the edges loose and looking more natural.

FINISHING THE QUILT

1. With the wool embellishments in place, add dimensional stitching and beading as desired.

2. Hand stitch the binding in place as described on page 31.

Adding to Your Bag of Tools

Working with wool and yarns provides many ways to add dimensional color and texture, and the fiber is so fun and easy to work with. Now that you've tried your hand at making wool flowers and roving gems, you'll enjoy creating more wooly treasures in all shapes and sizes. Have fun making them shine and twinkle in the light! I can almost guarantee that felting wool will be near the top of your list of favorite techniques found in your bag of tools.

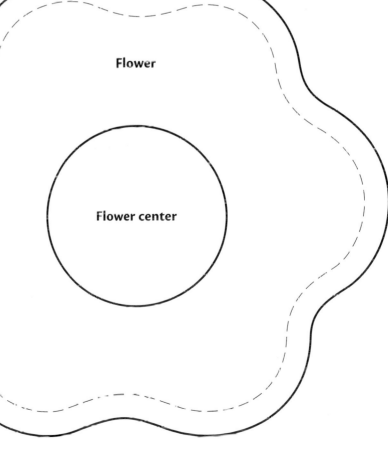

Flower

Flower center

Background pattern
Enlarge 333%.

HOW TIME FLIES
paper and lutradur

Memories stir the heart and are a culmination of all that we are. In the introduction, I shared some of my favorite fabric memories. Warm, fuzzy feelings regarding fabric are pretty common among us fabricaholics, and many of you may recognize some of the symptoms in yourself. You'll notice the symptoms when you touch certain fabrics or see a certain style of clothing.

And of course everyone has photos that help kick-start memories and tug on the heartstrings. This little quilt was designed around a black-and-white photo taken by one of my sisters. She remembers taking the picture with her Brownie camera, and I remember that autograph hound dog. Here I've created a new fabric memory with a tinted copy of the original photograph and a product called Lutradur. I encourage you to try this for yourself.

Finished size: 16" x 16"

PAPER AND LUTRADUR EMBELLISHMENTS

The centerpiece of this quilt is the old family photo. There are many ways to print photos on fabric, but I chose to print on paper and enclose the copy in a laminating pouch. These are readily available at office-supply stores and can be used for any type or shape of paper you want to attach to a quilt. The photo is centered on a Lutradur base. This is a fabulous material—one that takes paint (and/or a variety of mediums) and stitching like it was designed for no other purpose (although it was originally created as a roofing product). The ease of these methods leaves you lots of time to add small, special extra details that bring a memory to new life.

MATERIALS FOR BACKGROUND QUILT

1 fat quarter of multicolored brown-and-rust fabric

1 fat quarter of rust cotton/silk blend fabric

¼ yard of fabric for basic binding

1 fat quarter of fabric for backing

18" x 18" piece of batting

Yarn for couching

MATERIALS FOR EMBELLISHMENTS

1 copy of your chosen photo

1 self-sealing laminating pouch, letter size (approximately 9" x 11½")

8" x 8" piece of 100g Lutradur*

Red, brown, and yellow Inktense pencils**

1" wide paintbrush

Water dish

*Available from quilt shops and online

**Available from art-supply stores

CUTTING

From each of the background fabrics, cut:
1 piece, 16½" x 16½"

STITCHING THE BACKGROUND QUILT

Enlarge the background pattern on page 71 and draw it to full size, 16½" x 16½". Follow the steps in "Cloud Fly-By" on page 22 to enlarge the pattern, prepare the fabric, and complete the construction of the quilt top. Use the trim diagram on page 69 when cutting away the pattern sections to prepare for

couching. Refer to "Couching and Quilting Basics" on page 27 to complete the background quilt and apply basic binding.

Trim diagram

MAKING THE LUTRADUR AND PHOTO EMBELLISHMENT

1. Print your photo onto bright white copy paper (minimum weight 24 lbs.). To fit the dimensions of the quilt, crop or trim the photo to measure 5½" x 5½". I chose an old family black-and-white photo and tinted it red, using Photoshop, before printing it out. You can use an original photo if you prefer, but for old family photos, it's best to use a copy rather than the original.

Here's my photo in black and white, and then tinted red for use on the quilt.

2. Pull open the self-sealing laminating pouch, remove the protective sheet, and place the photo inside, leaving at least 1" around on all sides. Firmly press the sheets together, following the manufacturer's instructions.

Remove the protective sheet from the laminating pouch and place the photo inside, leaving at least 1" on all sides.

3. Using scissors or a rotary cutter, trim the laminated photo to 6½" x 6½", leaving ½" on all sides of the photo.

4. To prepare the Lutradur, color the entire sheet using the three colors of Inktense pencils. The colors will mix together nicely once they're painted over with water.

Use Inktense pencils to color the Lutradur sheet.

5. Paint over the piece using the paintbrush and water. Any brush will work, but I like a sponge brush for this task. Let dry completely. Once dry, the color is permanent.

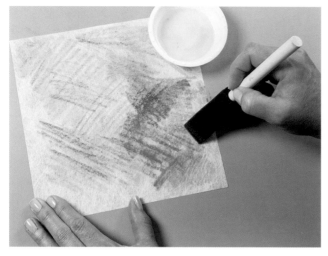

Blend the Inktense colors with water and allow to dry.

6. Center the prepared photo on the painted side of the Lutrador. With decorative thread, machine stitch the laminated pouch about 1/16" from the outside edge of the photo, stitching through the laminate and the Lutradur.

7. With the photo embellishment stitched to the Lutradur base, trim the combined piece to fit the center of the quilt, which is 7" x 7".

8. Using decorative thread, machine stitch the center photo embellishment into place. I stitched around the photo three times. You can use some of the decorative stitches on your machine if you like.

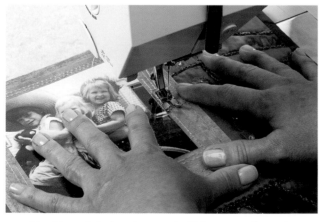

Machine stitch the photo embellishment to the quilt.

FINISHING THE QUILT

1. With the photo embellishment in place, add any additional stitching and beading.

2. Hand stitch the binding in place as described on page 30.

Adding to Your Bag of Tools

I hope that you have a lot of fun adding paper memorabilia, photos, and other flat items (whether laminated or not) to your quilts. I know you'll love playing with color on Lutradur to create beautiful, whimsical, and unique embellishments all your own.

Though there are many, many more embellishment opportunities to be explored, you now have quite a few useful new implements for your bag of tools. Reach in, grab them, and have a good time building your personal stepping stones.

Background pattern
Enlarge 222%.

DESIGNING REALITY,
simplified and stylized

Art is part of the daily experience of being human that takes form as we imitate our surroundings—creating and arranging the color and sounds of our lives while seeking to fulfill our heart's desire.

With all of the artistic arranging and rearranging we do, we naturally gravitate toward the things that attract us as individuals. Art is personal, and what catches me, hook, line, and sinker as they say, may not be what catches you. As we begin to consciously design, we strive to order various elements around us with consideration to balance, unity, and dominance, all the while fulfilling our need for self-expression.

I'm drawn to clean, simple lines, pure color, a bit of sparkle, and I enjoy looking to nature for inspiration. But, how does one go about finding clean and simple when looking at a busy scene? Even as I write this, I can still hear my high-school art teacher saying, "Simplify, simplify, simplify."

PEELING AWAY THE DETAILS

Simplify means to make simpler, less complex, or easier. To accomplish this, my art teacher encouraged us to look at our subjects, see the subject, identify its most important elements, and then draw the subject removing any nonessential elements.

As you simplify, peel away details to the point where the subject takes on an appearance that closely resembles its natural state. You can continue the peeling-away process until all that remains is the skeleton of the original.

By simplifying the subject to its most essential elements, we remove visual clutter that can be distracting and that can make it difficult to identify the subject. After the simplifying process is under way, we get to a point where we need to select and visually order one or more elements. Designing begins when we place and order these simplified elements into a predetermined space. This is usually a rectangular shape, but whatever the size or shape, it's known as the format.

Choosing a pleasing format for a particular subject is very important. Even when using the basic rectangle, the ideal position for your design may be horizontal rather than vertical. But, don't be afraid to try something out of the ordinary—a circle, square, or maybe even a wildly free-shaped format.

Moving from Realistic to Abstract

Realistic images provide a representation of your subject as it may be found and seen in the physical world. They're pictorial in nature and are highly recognizable by the viewer.

As we continue to simplify basic structural elements, the original subject may change in size, shape, or position. This creates a stylized version of the original image, and though the scene takes on a different appearance, the original object remains recognizable.

By continuing to simplify, the shapes of the original image naturally begin to metamorphose into basic geometric shapes. These new shapes may show very little similarity to the original subject, and are called abstract.

The photo of cacti on the facing page was taken on a trip to Catalina Island. I marked it to indicate the various shapes that can be used to simplify it. The illustrations then show further stages of simplifying.

Simplify by highlighting the basic outlines of the shapes.

Take the Simplification Challenge

I'm sure you have wonderful photos taken on fun excursions with family and friends. For this challenge, pull some of these photos out and, using copies of the photos themselves, try simplifying the images. Simplify, simplify, simplify, peeling away all the details. Play with the size, shape, and position of some of the simplified images you come up with. Keep going and have fun coming up with wild combinations that may just turn into your next quilt.

PLACING SIMPLIFIED ELEMENTS

The process of simplification helps to move your design from reality, to representational, to stylized, and on to abstraction. When you begin the placement of your design elements within the selected format, the fun really starts. Read on for some basic design principles that will allow you to show your subject within the selected format to its best advantage.

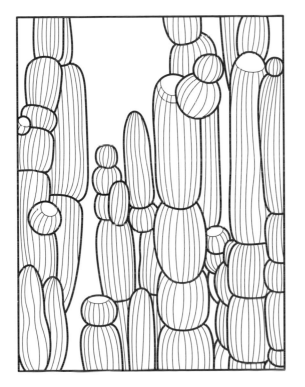

DESIGNING REALITY, SIMPLIFIED AND STYLIZED

Subject or Focus

There should always be a center of interest or focus for your design. This presents the subject as the design, rather than having it become part of the background or part of a pattern.

- Placing a subject off center will create a natural balance to your design.

- Place your subject in the center if you're striving to obtain a highly symmetrical or formal design.

- Plan your design so that your subject has opportunities to interact with the edges of the selected format.

- Position the main subject so that it draws the viewer's attention toward the focal point of the design. The main subject should not face away from the design area.

- When a subject represents a moving object, place open space in front of the object. This gives the impression that the object is ready to move into that space.

- Follow the "rule of odds." An odd number of objects are more interesting than an even number; so if you plan to use more than one object in your picture, choose an arrangement with at least three objects and odd numbers after that.

Ground or Background

To keep the viewer engaged it's important to consider the movement of the objects within your chosen format and background.

- To keep a viewer's eye moving across the entire piece, use closely related adjacent shapes, flowing lines or gradations of color. These will smoothly carry the viewer's gaze from one area to another, allowing each element in the work to be seen.

- Break the space up using unequal parts. Avoid exact bisections of the space.

- Place the horizon lines higher or lower than the middle of your selected format. This will spatially emphasize either the sky or the ground, and the horizon line will not divide the artwork into two equal parts.

FINDING INSPIRATION

As you try out new methods and new materials, your eyes and imagination will also begin to wander into new areas. This will open up many new horizons to be explored.

Look for the extraordinary in the everyday events and happenings in your life. Be a bit more adventurous in your search for embellishments. Take a left turn instead of that usual right-hand turn. Who knows what wonderful things you'll find!

ARTIST'S gallery

My journey as a quilt artist has been and continues to be a fun roller-coaster ride that's filled with amazing highs and exhilarating curves. Many of the quilts I'm sharing here in the gallery are from the time when I was moving away from traditional quilt work. As I explored opportunities to play with color, construction methods, and of course embellishment, I used my favorite motif, the raven. I hope you enjoy my raven quilts and the exploration they represent as part of my journey. Though my current work does not have the overt raven focus of my earlier quilts, he's there in spirit and continues to provide opportunity for me to explore.

Flight Plan; 37" x 32"

February's Flight IV; 40" x 40"

February's Flight V; 30" x 35"

New Beginnings II; 29" x 41"

Close; 24" x 48"

Closer; 24" x 48"

Closest; 24" x 48"

Earth Raven Creates; 45" x 45"

Don't Think Yourself in a Jail; 33" x 24"

They Think They're So Smart; 45" x 45"

Riding the Thermals; 45" x 47"

Eyes Skyward; 32" x 28"

Wintergreen Path; 32" x 45"

GUEST ARTISTS' gallery

Sharing is a powerful gift, and the quilt artists that appear here are sharing works, created on their own, while using one or more of the various embellishment methods found in this book. I love their choices of materials and seeing how they used them to create these wonderful quilts. I hope they'll inspire you to take the methods that I've presented in this book, throw them into your bag of tools, and use them when creating your own unique quilts.

Sweet Adelaide, Australia; 18" x 24". Made by Analee Perica.

Walking through the Forest; 17" x 18". Made by Cindy Rinne.

Getting into Shape; 22½" x 17". Made by David Charity.

Comforts; 5" x 7". Made by Ellenina Gaston.

Bird in Tree with Leaves Asking for Peace #4; 12" x 16". Made by Joanell Connelly.

Water's Edge; 14" x 22". Made by Jeanette Kelly.

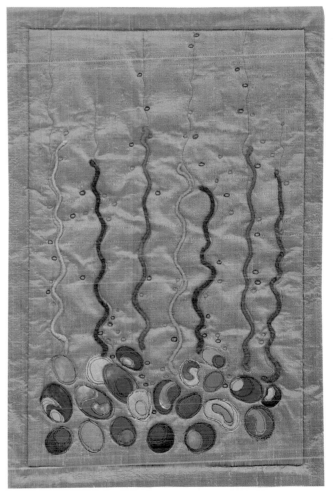

Life Force; 16" x 24". Made by Jeanette Kelly.

Kingdom of the Robber Bird; 18" x 24". Made by Josephine Jarvis.

Who Do Voodoo?; 30" x 30". Made by J. P. Griffith.

Flowers in Wonderland; 13⅝" x 16¾". Made by Mary Ellen Sakai.

Nature's Seasons; 12" x 17".
Made by Marcia Ann Kuehl.

Family Corvidae; 17½" x 20". Made by Stacy Hurt.

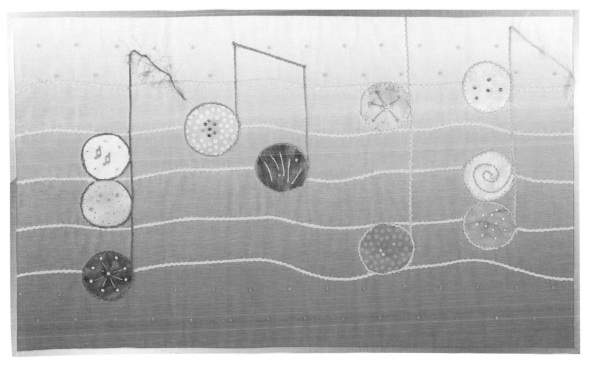

Bright Jazz; 18" x 30". Made by Marilyn Kirschen.

Pinkle Sunshine; 45" x 36". Made by Muna Elias.

Poway "B"; 27" x 22". Made by Mary Tabar.

Poway "T"; 27" x 22". Made by Mary Tabar.

It Felt Like an Approaching Storm; 17" x 17½". Made by Patricia Charity.

RESOURCES

FABRIC

Robert Kaufman Fabrics
Box 59266, Greenmead Station
Los Angeles, CA 90059-0266
800-877-2066
www.robertkaufman.com

THREADS AND YARNS

Presencia USA
PO Box 2409
Evergreen, CO 80437-2409
866-277-6364
www.threads.com

Superior Threads
87 East 2580 South
St. George, UT 84790
800-499-1777
www.superiorthreads.com

WOOL FELT, WOOL ROVING

Bird Brain Designs
3684 Shoreline View Way
Kelseyville, CA 95451
800-807-6420
www.birdbraindesigns.net

EMBELLISHMENTS, ANGELINA FIBERS

Soft Expressions
1230 N. Jefferson Street, Suite M
Anaheim, CA 92807
888-545-8616
www.softexpressions.com

LUTRADUR

The Quilter's Studio
1090 Lawrence Drive, Unit 101
Newbury Park, CA 91320
805-480-3550
www.quiltersstudio.com

YARN AND EMBELLISHMENTS

Purl in the Pines
2109 N. Fourth Street
Flagstaff, AZ 86004
928-774-9334
www.purlinthepines.com

GENERAL ART SUPPLIES: PAPERS, BRUSHES, PAINTS, AIR-DRY CLAY

Art Supply Warehouse
6672 Westminster Blvd.
Westminster, CA 92804
800-854-6467
www.artsupplywarehouse.com

Blick Art Materials
P.O. Box 1267
Galesburg, IL 61402-1267
800-828-4548
www.dickblick.com

About the AUTHOR

Photo by Carlo Parducho

After 20 years in the corporate world, Rose Hughes jumped into her quilt-art life in 2003 and has never looked back. She's always loved photography, and that love serves her well as she continues along her journey working with fabric to create landscapes in fiber.

Since the publication of her book, *Dream Landscapes: Artful Quilts with Fast-Piece Appliqué* (Martingale & Company, 2008), she has been traveling, providing entertaining and educational lectures, and having a great time teaching. She teaches her Fast-Piece Appliqué technique (of course), but she also has a strong lineup of workshops covering other topics, including design, fabric painting, color, and embellishments.

Rose has been quilting since 1991, and she continues to pursue her own art forms. Many of her quilts have been accepted in juried exhibitions nationwide, and her works are included in numerous corporate and private art collections. She is an active member of Studio Art Quilt Association and is the founder of Quilts on the Wall: Fiber Artists in Southern California, an organization that will soon be celebrating 15 years of educating quilters and the public about quilt art.

There's More Online!

Find out more about Rose and see additional photos of her work at www.rosehughes.com.

Find other great books on quilting and more at www.martingale-pub.com.